Published by TGM Ltd

Design and photograph restoration by Mike Lavender.

TGM Ltd B93 8NE   01564 770121   E-mail tgm@clara.co.uk

Brum Rocked!

Laurie Hornsby

Edited by Mike Lavender

Special thanks to:
Phil Ackrill, Mick Bakewell, Bob Barratt, Harry Belcher, Tim Bellamy, Brian Betteridge, Brenda Bosworth, Chuck Botfield, Roger Bruce, John Butler, Alan Buxton, Jim Carr, Johnny Carroll, Dave Carter, John Carter, Carl Chinn, Wilf Clare, Andy Coleman, Brian Collins, Jill Collins, John Collins, Pat Connolly, Neil Cressin, Mair Davies, Joe Dignam, Kevin Duffy (Erdington Library), Mel Edwards, Josey Elson, Birmingham Evening Mail, John Gibbins, Steve Gibbons, Robbie Harper, Paul Hewitt, Steve Horton, Ray Humphries, Bill Hunt, Mick Jones, Stasia Kennedy, Grant Kierney, Danny King, Pete Knight, Johnny Landon, Mel Lees, Gerry Levene, Greg Masters, Alan Meredith, Dave Mountney, Johnny Neal, Brian Newman, Jimmy Onslow, Roger Ottley, Tommy Owen, Keith Powell, Mark Raymond, Joe Regan, Euan Rose, John Rowlands, Dennis Ryland, Keith Seeley, Brian Sharp, Mike Sheridan, Bob Sheward, Keith Smart, John Stafford, Adrian Styles, Paul Taylor (Birmingham Central Library), Bobby Thomson, Holly Tooze, Ray Trilloe, Dezi Vyse, Terry Wallace, Clint Warwick, Pat Wayne, Peter Wilkins, Graham Williams, Pete Worrall, Nigel Wright, Rodney Wright & Brian Yeates.

*F*ORWORD

Laurie Hornsby is a bloke whose soul is filled with the sounds of Brum. With an ear echoing to our sayings, with a heart thumping to the rhythm of our city and with a mind always thoughtful to our characters, Laurie is the man who has become the acclaimed balladeer of working-class Birmingham. Why? Because his songs reach into the innermost thoughts and feelings of his fellow Brummies and make us want to join him on his journeys to bygone days. Through his meaningful lyrics Laurie Hornsby has proven his power as a writer, a power which he shows to the full in this first book. It is a wonderful evocation of those years from the mid 1950s to the mid 1960s when a new music rocked the land. Laurie's writing is pacy, it is insightful, it is knowledgeable and it pounds with the folk and music about which he is writing. Rightfully, Merseyside has been acclaimed for the part its people played in the development of pop music. Now, thanks to Laurie Hornsby, Birmingham too can be placed firmly in the fore of the pulsating, new force which transformed the music of a nation.

Carl Chinn

Lecturer in Modern History and Community Historian at the University of Birmingham

W ELL IT'S ONE FOR THE MONEY . . .

Chapter One

It's hard to imagine that once upon a time there was no rock 'n' roll. Throughout the towns and cities of Great Britain, people were getting back to normal following the second world war and its effects on their social life.

With the mid 1950s approaching, folks, without realising it, began to look for a better standard of living. A fair few families had a television which actually beamed pictures of clay potters working their wheels and a game show where a panel of middle class celebrities would endeavour to guess the occupations of visiting tradesmen by way of a 'piece of mime please'.

But it was the wireless that was the provider of good solid family entertainment. Over the airwaves came songs that told of doggies for sale in windows, exactly where to find a baby's dimple and the perils of tangoing with an Eskimo. Fathers and grandfathers would sit

Hedley Ward Orchestra at Wolverhampton Civic Hall

proudly in their corner chairs as their teenaged offspring swooned to the emotionally charged melody, 'Oh Mein Papa' that rasped from the horn of a golden trumpet. Music was proper again. The Yanks had gone home.

Now there were proper tunes with proper words, performed by proper artistes with perfect diction.

Okay, Johnny Ray was a 'bit of a jitterbugger' who used to cry on cue, but he meant well — he was a proper star.

In Birmingham, parents could rest easy in the knowledge that their sons and daughters were dancing to proper bands with proper musicians. At the **Grand Casino**, Corporation Street there was the **Teddy Foster Band** with Birmingham's 'Mr Sinatra' — **Kenny Day**, and **Manny Berg and his Music** whilst the **West End** would feature the **Sonny Rose Orchestra** with **Warren Dorsey**, and with **Colin Hulme** tinkling the ivories at **Tony's Ballroom** in Hurst Street, a good time was guaranteed for all.

The suburbs also provided first class entertainment of the highest order. At **Saltley Baths**, **Hedley Ward and his Orchestra** would serenade the night away, as would **Cliff Deeley** at **Nechells Baths**, and over in Smethwick at **Thimblemill Baths**, folks would swoon to the music of **Lee Lombard**. **Vernon Adcock** was at the **Masque**, **Henry Goodall** at the **Springfield**, **Billy Mortiboys and his Black and White Dance Band** were at the **Wolseley**, Drews Lane, **Fred Edwards** was at the **Swan**, Yardley, **Charlie Simpson** and his orchestra were residing at the **Ritz**, Kings Heath, and with **Jimmy Cousins** at the **Morris Club**, Alum Rock, Brum was, as far as music was concerned, in safe hands. The Yanks had gone home and taken their jitterbugging with them!

In 1954, a record appeared on the British charts by Bill Haley and his Comets. 'Shake, Rattle and Roll' caused quite a stir on the dance floors across Brum. Long gone memories of GIs came flooding back as people once again did the 'jitterbug'.

Seated in the corner, father, smoking his pipe, raised an eyebrow as from the wireless came that rockabeatin' rhythm and that crazy lyric — 'Get out that kitchen and rattle them pots and pans!' Father smiled to see his kids moving to the beat. It was harmless enough. Perhaps he wouldn't have smiled so broadly had the Brunswick Record Company not insisted on Mr Haley revising the original lyric, 'Get out that bed and

Lee Lombard at Thimblemill Baths 1955

wash your face and hands', suggesting a rather more seedy lifestyle to mid 50s Britain. Father smiled and puffed on his pipe. Life was good.

It was 1955 and cinemas were doing great business. Everyone loved the pictures. If you weren't staying in or dancing, you went to the pictures. Glenn Ford was a 'hot' movie star at the time and his film in '55 was 'Blackboard Jungle', which dealt with problems between kids and parents in middle America.

The film was a great success at the box office, firstly because it was a good film, and secondly because as the credits rolled, so a Bill Haley recording — 'Rock Around the Clock' — played over the titles causing, as newspapers reported, teenagers to 'rip up' cinema seats. This was of course, gross exaggeration, but as a result of the publicity, the recording found itself, in late November '55, on top of the British hit parade.

Charlie Simpson

As New Years Eve revellers sang out Auld Lang Syne in Chamberlain Square that last night of 1955, how could they have known the effect that 'Rock Around the Clock' would have on their lives? As father tore round the neighbourhood at midnight on that very evening, clutching a piece of coal in one hand whilst clinging to his pipe with the other, how could he have had any idea of what lay ahead? Rock 'n' roll was, as far as he was concerned, mumbo jumbo music that had no place in society. It was a nine day wonder. The kids would soon tire of all this jitterbugging and get back to proper dancing to proper tunes with proper words that you could hear and understand. Rock 'n' roll would be all over and out of the way in a few weeks.

Elvis Presley

Then it happened. A young hillbilly kid by the name of Elvis Presley hit the charts with 'Heartbreak Hotel'. Father winced as his youngsters imitated this so called entertainer by gyrating their hips and snarling out nonsense lyrics about bell hops and desk clerks dressed in black. Britain went wild as images filtered through, via newspapers, of this stunningly handsome youth dressed in a most outrageous style, driving infatuated young ladies to the point of hysteria.

Grandfathers pleaded for calm as happy households became wildly disrupted. Arguments were raging over the volume of the radio or the wind-up gramophone when the record by this Elvis Presley fellow was played. The BBC announced that normal service would resume as soon as possible. Elvis took up the challenge and delivered his knockout punch by releasing his second recording from which the world has never fully recovered — *'Blue Suede Shoes'*.

Father picked up his tobacco tin and retired to the parlour. The Yanks were back, if not in the flesh, then in spirit. The King was dead. Long live the King!

Chapter Two

MIGHTY GOOD ROAD TO RIDE

This rock 'n' roll music wasn't anything new as far as **Arthur Benwell** was concerned. At his home in Theodore Street just off Summer Lane, Arthur had been receiving American blues and soul records by mail order since the days of his early teens in '52. The parcels came from Mr Albert Schultz, of West 14th Street in New York, and they always arrived marked 'educational'!

These 'educational' parcels contained recordings by such artistes as Big Joe Turner, Smiley Lewis and Eugene Church and gave Arthur access to material that performing pop artistes would have given their right arms for. Consequently, when Arthur began working himself as a solo artiste he was a great success. Singing for the collection at the end of the evening in pubs like the **Gunmakers** in the Jewellery Quarter, he accompanied himself on guitar, using the famous three chords that he'd managed to master. Doing songs like Big Joe's 'Lipstick, Powder and Paint', it quickly became apparent that here was a performer with something to offer that was a little special. In short Arthur was, as the Yanks put it, 'hip to the tip'.

Tex Detheridge and the Gators at the Mermaid, Sparkhill

For some time in early '56, **Dennis Detheridge** had been regarded as Sparkhill's Hank Williams. Hank, the legendary American country singer/writer died aged just twenty-nine in 1952, leaving behind such gems as 'Your Cheatin' Heart'. Abandoning Dennis for the more trendy name 'Tex' he assembled the **Gators** as his backup band. From Hall Green came **Brian Sharpe** on drums.

From Lakey Lane and with guitars came brothers **Geoff** and **Maurice Taylor** and from Sparkhill came the one-eyed wonder of the steel guitar, **Jimmy Wilde**.

Together, **Tex Detheridge and the Gators** created the true atmosphere of a Texas 'honky-tonk' every Saturday at the **Mermaid**, Stratford Road, and on Sundays the world would stand still on Bilberry Hill. That's the hill at the foot of Rose Hill at the Lickeys, where Tex and the boys would treat dancers to a hoe-down in the **Bilberry Tea Rooms**. Ladies skirts rode up high as their gentlemen partners twirled them around the floor whilst showing off their own fancy footwork, and as they danced, so Tex and the boys would sing 'Hey good Lookin'' and the crowd would holler back "What you got cookin'!"

There was plenty of jambalaya cookin' at Shirley Carnival in the summer '56 as skiffle outfits were pitched against each other in a 'battle of the bands' contest. Come the evening and the grand final, the **Blackcats** and the **Aces** were judged runners up to **Tony's Skiffle Band,** but when it was discovered that young **Dave Carter** had only appeared in the final, and not the afternoon heat, **Tony's Skiffle Band** were disqualified.

From the Hedley Ward Orchestra sprang the 'hip' minded **Hedley Ward Trio**. The threesome were managed by their mentor Mr Hedley Ward, and from his offices in the Great Western Building in Livery Street he guided them through the minefield that the music business had become.

A handsome young Small Heath man, John Neal, worked by day at the family's scrap paper business, but at night John became **Johnny Neal**, dynamic pop singer. He'd tried his hand as an entertainer back in '53, when, following a few words of advice from **Kenny Day** at the **Casino**, John, at the local hop held at **Ada Road School**, Small Heath, performed an impression of Billy Daniels doing 'That Old Black Magic'. "But," says Johnny, "I knocked the corners

The trio - bassist and lead vocalist Derek Franklin, guitarist Jack McKechnie, and Bob Carter on the ivories, actually recorded an early version of 'Rock Around the Clock' complete with three part harmony for the Melodisc label. With a style reminiscent of the King Brothers, the Hedley Ward Trio enjoyed tremendous success on the variety circuit. Beryl Reid, the comedienne who portrayed the Brummie wench Marlene in her stand up routine became Mrs Derek Franklin

ATV presenter Noele Gordon and resident band the Jerry Allen Trio — a legend in their own Lunchbox

off my performances when I was called up to serve with the 9th Queens Royal Lancers and learned my trade with the Regiment Band." An appearance on the **Carroll Levis Discoveries Show** at the **Hippodrome** brought him to the attention of **Fred Wilby**, a talent scout for the recently launched **ATV** in Aston, and Johnny, in '56, at the age of twenty-one appeared on **Lunchbox**, an early afternoon show presented by **Noele Gordon**, with the **Jerry Alan Trio** providing musical accompaniment.

"I was also voted 'Midlands King of Song'," laughs Johnny as he remembers singing on BBC's **Come Dancing**, from the **Casino**, "and **Pat Howard**, from Malmesbury Road, Small Heath, who sang at the **Gay Tower Ballroom** in Edgbaston, was voted queen."

Midlands King & Queen of Song with Teddy Foster at the Casino, 1956

On leaving school in '55, **Ray Trilloe**, of William Street, just at the bottom of Lozells Road, began working at **R G Sutcliffe**, a record shop on Lodge Road. With pop music growing in popularity by the day, he wanted to be part of it. On buying his first guitar for two pounds and ten shillings he realised that he couldn't even tune it, never mind play it. His prayers were answered when he met up with **Albert Eccles**, who lived not too far away, in Alma Street. Now Albert could not only tune up, but he could play a few chords and sing a fair song.

Albert had been born and spent his earlier years in Wilton Street, Aston, where he sang in the local church choir and bugled for the Boys' Brigade. In his mid-teens he developed a disease in his left ankle bone.

"They had me in the General," said Albert. "They reckoned the bottom half of my leg would have to go, but they took out the ankle bone and I've been okay ever since!"

A mate of his, **Alan Hancox**, also from Alma Street, would be a regular bedside visitor to Albert during his hospitalisation, and would bubble with enthusiasm about the new hobby that he was pursuing. Alan had discovered the joy of rock 'n' roll music and had actually purchased a guitar.

To relieve the chronic boredom, Albert asked his parents if, on their next visit, they could maybe bring him a guitar instead of a bunch of grapes. Not only did Albert receive his first guitar, but also a tuition book, and after a week or so of ripping his fingers to pieces on the wire strings, Albert finally gave a recital to the fellow patients and staff of ward 11, accompanied by the chap in the next bed blowing away on harmonica, whilst a notice, *nil by mouth* hung from his bedpost.

The Rainbow Boys at the Co-Op Rooms, Lozells

In '56, guitarists Ray Trilloe, Albert Eccles and Alan Hancox were joined by **Tony Luckman**, **Mick Cope** on washboard, and on tea chest bass came **David Rainbow**. They called themselves the **Rainbow Boys**. Immediately they set about rehearsing, practising until their fingers were sore and sometimes bled. With heads held high they began venturing out to perform at the **Roebuck**, Soho Hill, the **Hare and Hounds**, Kingstanding, the **Golden Cross**, Aston and the **Crown and Cushion**, Perry Barr, counting out the copper coins (from the whip-round) on the tea chest. Finally they landed their prize engagement — a residency every Saturday evening at the **Co-Op Rooms**, Lozells Road, where Ray's mother was the caretaker. It seemed in next to no time the boys were on stage at the prestigious **Dudley Hippodrome** as one of **Caroll Levis'** discoveries. Quite a few appearances at **Birmingham Town Hall** followed and Ray's most treasured recollection is a show the **Rainbow Boys** performed for children at the **Royal Orthopaedic Hospital** in Northfield.

Hopping off the No. 14 bus at Great Lister Street Nechells, straight into the New Inns and armed with guitars would be Harry Belcher, his brother-in-law Rex and Joe Dignam. These lads were the Tiger Sharks and they would serve up their own brand of gritty skiffle songs that had been especially honed to suit the tastes of gas works employees who frequented the bar

The **MEM** in Reddings Lane had its own workers' social club that would have, as its resident outfit, the **Mike Jacks Trio**. With Mike on piano, there was **Ron Hughes** on bass and, from the **Gators**, MEM employee **Brian Sharpe** on drums.

Mike Jacks Trio at the MEM Club, Reddings Lane, Tysley, 1956

Johnny Neal & the Houn'dogs

"So one night," says Brian, "**Johnny Neal** saunters into the club. We knew him vaguely and he sang a few numbers with us. Rock 'n' roll was just kicking off and Johnny had got whatever it took. White socks, brothel creepers, the lot! He could also whack out a great song!" Johnny Neal put in with the lads there and then and, after a session at **Stella's Bar** (which was actually the function room over the top of the **Avenue** pub in Aston, and a haunt for local musicians) Mr Neal and his associates were joined by **Alan Jaeger** on sax, and an old schoolmate of Johnny's on guitar, **Graham 'Eddie' Pebble**. Elvis's Houn'dog was the hit song of the week and the inspiration to name the band, **Johnny Neal and the Houn'dogs**.

"We were there at the start," says Johnny. "One of the first — although I do recall another great outfit kickin' around — **Frankie and the Hi Cards**."

When the **Houn'dogs** appeared at the **Dog and Partridge**, Yardley Wood, they experienced hysteria for the first time as the audience went wild for this 'new' music. Shortly after this, Johnny and the boys performed 'Rudy's Rock', a Bill Haley's Comets number, at the **Casino**, with Alan playing sax, whilst lying flat on his back. Ron began clambering over his double bass as Mike, wearing a crash helmet, played piano with one foot. "The Casino crowd went bananas but we never had a fee," explained **Johnny Neal**. "The gaffer, Albert Archer, gave us a ten bob note and told us to have a drink."

In Grange Road, Small Heath, **Wilf Clare's** mother allowed her parlour to be used for skiffle sessions by her son's outfit, the **Gladiators**. Along with Wilf were **Geoff Stokes**, **Archie Edwards** and

Wally who put in a performance at the **Gunmakers Arms** for a fee of 7/6d each and at the **Custard House**, Blake Lane, the **Noisy Boys** were at it. Everyone was having a ball. As the bands rocked so the dancers bopped away their blues. Everyone was young and foolish and the world was alive and wide open for the taking.

Wilf Clare & the Gladiators in Wilf's Mom's parlour, 1956

Out in the sticks, the youths of Coleshill were boppin' at the **Shustoke Village Hall** to the **Nighthawks**, from Castle Bromwich, who cost the organisers fifteen shillings for their appearance. With **Bob Sheward** laying down the rock-a-billy beat, strumming and singin' the blues were **Johnny Hodgkinson**, **Ricky**, and brothers **Ken** and **Keith Horden**. The **Nighthawks** were real heart throbs and provided ample fodder for the elder members of Coleshill Women's Institute to natter about for the following few months.

From Havelock Road in Saltley, just behind the Amateur Gardeners' Club, sprang the **Corsairs**. **Tommy Owen**, **Frankie Beeson**, **Brian Biggs** and **Alan Hingley** were joined by **Johnny Harris** and **Garth**

The Nighthawks at Shustoke Village Hall

The Corsairs at
East Birmingham Trades
& Labour Club 1957

Gene Vincent

Quirke from Highfield Road and together they introduced their own special approach to skiffle to the astonished members of the **East Birmingham Trades and Labour Club.**

The British had answered the American invasion with a tiny Glaswegian fellow, Lonnie Donegan, who sang 'train' songs about travelling on the 'Rock Island Line' to 'Cumberland Gap' with a hobo called 'Lost John'. Using simple chords on a guitar, with a rhythm strummed out on a washboard, this skiffle, as it was known, gave lads who had up until then been totally ignorant about music and its structure, a chance to be creative and develop performing skills.

Elvis had done it. There was a lad who wore a leg iron and, dressed in leather, sang the most absurd lyric to ever be recorded on wax. Be Bop a Lula! I ask you! *Be Bop a Lula!* And it was a smash hit! If this chap Gene Vincent could crack it — if Elvis could crack it — if a chap from Glasgow could crack it — then why not somebody from Birmingham?

Chapter Three

SURE LIKE TO BALL . . .

The palm trees weren't exactly swaying that particular Saturday afternoon in Summer Lane, but Spring was in the air and also in **Arthur Benwell**'s step. He'd spent his lunchtime jiving at the **Grand Casino**, Corporation Street — and why not? He was a keen dancer, indeed his brother Jim, was a professional instructor and Arthur, if you'll pardon the pun, could have followed in his brother's footsteps if the rock 'n' roll bug hadn't engulfed his system. It was his some-what regular Saturday routine. He'd return home to Theodore Street, then after a cup of tea, saunter up the 'Lane' and along Alma Street to Lozells Road, where stood **Haslucks** record shop. That's where Arthur, if he'd had a good week on the dogs, would buy a couple of rhythm and blues records to add to his collection. As he strolled he could hear the sound of guitars being strummed and a couple of voices echoing around a courtyard. Arthur stopped, listened, and was impressed. So much so that he introduced himself as a performer with a repertoire of quality rock 'n' roll songs. One of the lads was **Alan Hancox**, who had been a member of the **Rainbow Boys**. They had disbanded because, as **Ray Trilloe** put it, "It wasn't the be-all and end-all." For Alan though, it was. Alan introduced his brother and fellow picker, **Brian**, and sang the praises of one **Albert Eccles** who was in the process of purchasing a *real* bass guitar.

Following a few rehearsals, it was clear to everyone that they had the makings of a professional band. What they needed was a profes-sional name. Arthur gave it serious thought. Being a cinema fanatic he'd fallen in love with the Alan Ladd character 'Shane'. He was also a keen fan of the writer Kingsley Amis. Arthur pondered, *Shane Kings-ley?* He shook his head and continued in deep thought. Although everyone called him Arthur, he'd actually been christened Daniel Arthur. Again he pondered — *Daniel? Danny, Danny Kingsley? Yes! Danny Kingsley! No! Hold it. Too long. Shorten it. Danny King? Yes!* **Danny King**!

Albert Eccles also liked the idea of adopting a professional name for himself. "Danny came up with it." said Albert. "I loved this cowboy on television. He was a big bloke, like me. He played the part of Cheyenne Bodie, but his real name was Clint Walker. So Danny King called me Clint. The surname Warwick seemed to roll off the tongue, so there I was, **Clint Warwick**. And the band? Well, being patriotic, we kept the royal theme and called ourselves the **Dukes**."

The **Avion Cinema** at Aldridge would hardly pass as rock 'n' roll heaven. Neither would the **Unity Club** in Summer Lane, but both of these establishments gave **Danny King and his Dukes** a chance to reign supreme, or at least experience the awesome task of facing an audience in their formative days. But face them they did, rockin' away the night with blistering versions of 'Honey Hush', 'Touch Me', and the mind-blowing 'Shufflin' the Gravel'.

Impromptu entertainment from Terry Wallace & John Badderick at the Metro-Cammel Works, Saltley, Christmas 1957

During a day-trip to Highley with his parents in the Spring of '57, **Terry Wallace**, from Nechells (and educated at Ellen Street school) experienced for the first time, the atmosphere of 'live' music. His Dad, in need of a pint, had steered the family to the **Ship** pub and it happened that a skiffle session was in progress. Terry watched open mouthed as a couple of local lads sang and strummed 'Don't You

Rock Me Daddy-O', and once back home, he set about forming his own outfit.

From the start Terry, with his pals **George Jenkins, John 'Bango' Badderick** and **Terry Smith** were called the **Vikings**, and their first appearance was at **Cromwell Street Working Men's Club**, Nechells, where the house microphone used to hang down from the ceiling and totally obscure the audience's view of the featured vocalist. As the Vikings' became more proficient, so the bookings came rolling in and most evenings at around six forty-five, the boys could be seen queuing, instruments in hand, for a number 8 or 43 bus to transport them on their next rock 'n' roll exploits.

Meanwhile, **Patrick Curley**, from Osler Street, Ladywood, and his school pal **Ray Vaughan**, from Monument Road, had completed their education at the Oratory. Patrick, or as he preferred, Pat, had demonstrated himself to be a possessor of a strong set of vocal 'pipes' as a member of the Oratory choir but with skiffle strengthening its grip on the nation in '57, such formal music was the last thing

Danny King & his Dukes

on his mind as he and Ray commenced work as waiters at the Grand Hotel, Colmore Row. As it happened, a fellow waiter, **Dave Husthwaite**, was a serious student of the guitar, quite advanced in fact, compared to other young hopefuls of the day, and once breakfast was dispensed with and the restaurant laid for lunch, out would come his guitar to accompany Pat on current songs of the day. Not to be outdone, Ray would grab the cutlery to provide percussion. Realising that they had the 'bones' of a skiffle outfit, Pat set about making a tea chest bass, and Ray wasted no time in investing in a washboard and thimbles. The news story of that time was the launching, by the RAF, of a bat-winged aircraft, the Delta, and so to be topical, if nothing else, the lads called themselves the **Deltas**, and Pat decided that a professional stage name was called for.

"My middle name is William, so I

wanted the initials PW." said Pat. "The name came immediately – **Pat Wayne** – nothing to do with John Wayne, although when I was loaded up with the crocks in the Grand restaurant, I did tend to walk like him!"

For teenagers in '57, the youth club was the place to be. Whatever the juvenile desired was at hand. There was ping-pong, orange squash by the bucketful and, with a little luck, a group to groove to. The **Deltas**, the **Noisy Boys** and the **Vikings** were around to perform at such clubs as the one held at **Blakenhale School**, Garretts Green, every Friday evening, where the band would arrive by bus, armed with their precious guitars, a snare drum and possibly one puny amplifier between them.

Ray Vaughan, the **Deltas'** washboardist, had a brother, **Wally**, who kept the **Nelson** pub, just off Spring Hill. Every Saturday evening, in the bar, **George Bennett** would play his accordion, whilst a young lad, **Tony Butler**, played a fair lick or two on guitar. The Deltas immediately 'poached' Tony with promises of money, pretty girls and all the adulation that went with being a member of the famous band!

In his black dinner jacket and dicky bow, **George Bennett** was an enterprising character of the day. Not only did he promote shows at **Birmingham Town Hall**, he was also a bit of a talent scout. He had discovered **Quinton Capers**, two bubbly girls from — you've

Pat Wayne & the Deltas

guessed it, Quinton. **Olive Gauntlet** and **Jill Collins** met at Four Dwellings school.

"We'd done a few old folks homes and a couple of weddings." recalls Olive. "We both were taught to play guitar by my Dad, and we did songs like 'Freight Train', and 'Railroad Bill'."

Rehearsals took place at the **Abbey Vaults**, Key Hill and with **George Bennett** handling the business for them, and changing their name to the **Quinteenoes**, Olive and Jill performed their routines at **Birmingham Town Hall**, **Digbeth Civic Hall**, **Solihull Carnival** and **Pype Hayes Park**, where Jill fondly remembers they appeared as support act to family favourites, the Beverly Sisters.

Olive & Jill –
the Quinteenoes at
Birmingham Town Hall

"We sang 'Bye Bye Love' as our last song," Jill goes on. "Me and Olive really really got going. I s'pose when they came on doing 'Sisters', it seemed a bit tame compared to us!"

Following one George Bennett show at Birmingham Town Hall, **Johnny Neal** had some explaining to do to the missus. June, John's wife, had just bought him a tie and he chose to wear it during his performance that night. Suddenly a girl rushed the stage and grabbed Johnny's tie, nearly choking him. However the girl fainted as she pulled Johnny's lips to hers and an ambulance was summoned. As the smelling salts took effect, the poor girl regained her marbles, but refused to leave the building without Johnny's tie.

"The wife went crazy when I told her about the tie. She refused to believe me. Accused me of all sorts of mischief!" laughs Johnny Neal. *"As if I would!"*

At five minutes past six every Saturday teatime, households throughout the land came to a standstill as the 'Six-Five Special' came down the line and onto their television screens. Fathers buried their heads in the Sports Argus as their teenaged offspring pranced around the living room to a former dance band trombonist turned professional teddy boy by the name of Don Lang, who, with his band the Frantic Five, belted out the show's signature tune, as the show's presenters — Jo Douglas, Pete Murray and ex-boxer Freddie Mills demonstrated the hand jive. So successful was the show, that the powers that be put it out on tour featuring two of the show's hottest acts, Jim Dale, who was high in the charts at the time with 'Be My Girl', and the Vipers, a skiffle group fronted by Wally Whyton, who had written and recorded 'Don't You Rock Me Daddy-O'. When the **Six Five Special** was staged at the **Birmingham Hippodrome**, also on the bill were Brummie outfits the **Vikings**, the **Deltas**, the **Five Cards** and a rock-a-billy band with a knockout name, **Tommy Hawk and the Hatchets**. Tommy (christened **Sidney Hawkes**) was a Harborne lad who could play his black rose guitar like there was no tomorrow. The audience went wild as local boy **Terry Wallace** joined the **Vipers** to sing 'Cumberland Gap', and when **Sonny Gauntlet** and **Johnny Robson** of the **Five Cards** broke into a chorus of the Six-Five Special all hell broke loose as the audience began to yell back "Over the points! Over the points!"

For the **Deltas**, in that summer of '57, success was only a bus ride away as Sunday mornings would see them boarding the Midland Red bus armed with guitars and washboard, bound for Worcester where they would make their way to the riverside, hop aboard a pleasure steamer and busk for the day. On arrival back at Worcester, **Pat Wayne** would pass amongst the passengers, rattling a beer tray that would soon be full of half crowns, two bobs and shillings. On one occasion, the trip had been a 'boster'. Great weather, great trippers and plenty of ale to help lubricate Pat's vocal chords. The tray was brimming with silver as Pat made it back to the performing area to be greeted by more ale. In order to pick up his drink, he balanced the tray on the rail. As he supped, so the boat rocked and over the side and into the Severn went the day's wages. Everyone laughed. Who

The Vikings at the Town Hall, and later that night . . .

cared? It was only money. The **Deltas** were back the following Sunday, but they kept Pat away from the ale!

At the tender age of fourteen, **Pete Worrall**, of Hansons Bridge Road Erdington, joined forces with another fourteen year old, **Robbie Harper** and his younger brother **Steve**, who were round the corner in Woodlands Farm Road. A neighbour of theirs, **David Austin** was 'a bit of a spark' and converted an old radio into an amplifier for them, and their guitars, purchased from **Sheldon Music** on the Coventry Road, had electric pickups made and fitted by **Arthur Matthews**, next to Smith's brew-

. . . the Five Cards

ery at Aston. Arriving at the **Apollo Cinema**, Tyburn Road, the boys announced themselves as the **Roller Coasters**, they won the confidence of the manager, who booked them for the Saturday morning matinees. In their black shirts with red sequins and 'RC' embroidered on their breast pockets, they were a great success. So much so that other cinemas engaged them for similar gigs. Being enterprising lads they saved a fortune on bus fares by cycling to the venues, having made pram-wheeled trailers for their equipment! The **Castle Cinema**, across from the **Bradford** pub, and the **Beaufort Cinema**, Ward End, were their destinations, as was the **Rock Cinema**, where, after their show, they would move on down to the **Penguin Cafe** to enjoy egg and bacon sandwiches and mugs of tea until the fifteen bob gig money was blown.

If the Roller Coasters had looked out of the Penguin Cafe window they would have probably seen the **Corsairs** struggling with their gear onto the number eight Inner Circle bus bound for the **Bristol Cinema** where **Tommy Owen**, having taken over the payments on **Alan Hingley**'s Valencia guitar, would perform a hip-swinging 'Baby I Don't Care' to the Lea Bank teenagers.

Johnny Neal and the Houn'dogs were now going over big with the Brummie jivers. **Pat Wayne** describes them as a great driving

rock 'n' roll combo. "I used to watch them at the **Crown**, Hill Street," recalls Pat. "They were the biz. Johnny and the lads used to really wallop it out in those days!"

The **Houn'dogs** also walloped it out over at the **Harlequin**, Shard End, and **Brian Sharpe**, always the showman, would be seated behind his drum kit wearing, in keeping with the **Houn'dog** theme, a pair of 'Deputy Dawg' floppy ears!

The Nignogs at St Stephen's Hall, Selly Park

The **Nignogs** didn't have floppy ears. In fact the **Nignogs** didn't have a floppy anything. They were just a bunch of lads in their mid-teens who were endeavouring to make it as a skiffle group. Put together by vocalist **Ray Humphries** (who has since dedicated his life to political correctness) the other **Nignogs** were: **Bob Bradley**, **Graham Buckingham** and **Malc 'the bones' Jones**. After intense rehearsals, the **Nignogs** were summoned to **St Stephen's Hall**, Pershore Road, for their debut performance.

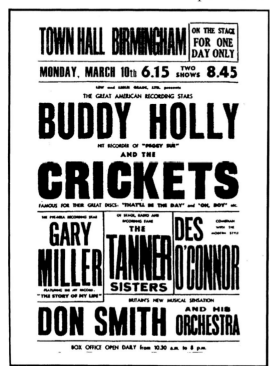

"We'd planned to carry the amplifier and tea chest bass from Bob's house in Cherrington Road, Stirchley and catch the bus down to Selly Park. But it was a pea-souper. Thick smog and the buses weren't running. So I humped the amplifier on my shoulder and set off down Pershore Road, stopping at the **Dogpool** for a welcome swifty. By the time I made the gig, my arms were dropping off, my chest was full of smog and I'd got a couple of pints of canal water inside me!" said Ray.

'To everything there is a season' according to The Book of Ecclesiastes and the Spring and Summer of '57 had been the season for skiffle. Basic as it was, it had proved to be a launch pad for more adventurous music. Showbiz waits for no one and fathers across the city had been correct in stating that skiffle was a fad that, like winter roses, would fade and die. However, as Autumn chilled the air, so on the airwaves, through the wireless and into our homes came the sound of the **Crickets**, a group of young Texans, performing an electrifying song, 'That'll Be the Day'. The actual construction of the song was the same as skiffle, the famous three chords, but phrased a little differently and with a blistering guitar introduction and solo that was to be initially a challenge, and then an incredible inspiration for all guitarists.

Washboards were returned to the brew-house, thimbles put back into the sideboard and fathers driven barmy by ambitious sons urging them to sign hire purchase agreements to buy guitars similar to the one used by the bespectacled leader of the Crickets — **Buddy Holly**.

Pat Wayne still chuckles whenever he recalls the day he managed to prise his father out of his chair and down to **Ridouts**, on Monument Road to sign on the dotted line, as guarantor for a Hofner President guitar. "It cost forty eight guineas! Not pounds but guineas! And how I was forced to vow, on bended knee, in that shop, in the presence of Mr Ridout, that I would honour, as a gentleman, my obligation of five shillings per week repayment."

Buddy Holly at Birmingham Town Hall, March, 1958

Although in '57, cinemas were still doing business, the writing was on the wall that television would soon be causing closures across the city. In Handsworth, rumours proved to be correct when the **Rookery** finally closed its doors. A few months later, thanks to an enterprising couple by the name of **Regan**, those doors re-opened — to the **Plaza Ballroom**. The Regans, old hands in the strict tempo business, were about to embrace the new music culture and become significant figures in the progress of rock music in Birmingham.

Chapter Four

Every Day it's Gettin' Closer...

Former schoolteacher **Mary Regan**, and her husband **Joe**, began their venture into the dancehall business in 1947 at the **Victoria**, (later re-named the **Garryowen**) in Wordsworth Road, Small Heath. Their clientele could enjoy regular helpings of strict tempo ballroom music courtesy of **Charlie Simpson and his Orchestra**. Soon Mary and Joe took another establishment under their wing, a sleepy Kings Heath snooker hall — the **Ritz** in York Road. The Regans turned it into a dancehall and gave it a kick-start by bringing over Charlie Simpson and his music as the main attraction.

The rhythm of life was demanding a step away from formality. The Regans, having the luck of the Irish with them, could sense it. They could smell success as it danced around on the winds of change that were blowing in from the other side of the Atlantic. Although they didn't know it at the time, it was the smell of rock 'n' roll.

Joe was no stranger to the dance-band environment. His father had led his own outfit in St Helens, Lancashire and although he hadn't inherited any musical talent, Joe had acquired the knowledge of stage presentation. As a youngster, he had set out for London and, whilst he didn't find streets paved with gold, he did find himself working as a page boy at the Cumberland Hotel.

"It was terribly la-di-da," he chuckled, recollecting days of permanent smiles and bowing and scraping to everyone that came through

Charlie Simpson & his Orchestra at the Ritz 1955

those grand revolving doors. His efforts to please were noted by the management of the Cumberland and young Joe Regan found himself acting as Master of Ceremonies at the 'toffee nosed' functions of pre-war London. Such experiences of microphone technique and clarity of speech were to prove invaluable to Joe in the years to come as he would proudly announce his artistes and forthcoming attractions in his own ballrooms – with just a trace of blarney!

"Elvis Presley changed everything," said Joe. "Can you imagine poor Charlie Simpson announcing a 'ladies excuse me' or a 'taxi quickstep' to a room full of teddy boys and their girls."

The **Ernie Lane** dance-band would quite regularly feature a four-teen year old vocalist from Nesbitt Grove, Bordsley Green by the name of **Keith Powell**. Keith could have probably made it as an actor. Indeed, at the Central Grammar school he'd demonstrated his per-forming skills by playing Waxford Squears Jnr in the school produc-tion of Nicholas Nickleby along with **Nicol Williamson**, now a highly successful actor, who played Keith's mother, and **Tony Gar-net**, now a leading film producer, who played Waxford Squears Snr! But it was as a singer that Keith would make his mark and those early days of crooning **Mack the Knife** to the quicksteppers were never to be wasted.

Show business had always figured in the Powell family and Keith was given maximum encouragement to continue the tradition. His fa-ther, Jim, one of thirteen from Erskine Sreet, Vauxhall, had surren-dered a promising boxing career in favour of a more glamorous occu-pation. He became a professional dancer at **Tony's Ballroom** in Hurst Street. In other words he was paid to dance with lonely ladies. A po-sition that most men would have killed for! He had also dabbled in promoting variety and had presented, to his credit, the Irish tenor, **Jo-seph Locke** at the **Custard House**, Blake Lane. It follows, of course, that Keith would figure prominently in his father's future presenta-tions.

Eighty, Blake Lane was the home of **Maurice 'Mo' Jones**, the leader of the **Noisy Boys** and the neighbours found them just that! As it happened, the **Custard House** was across the road and pro-vided a perfect rehearsal room, and at the bottom of Blake Lane, on Bordesley Green, was a record shop belonging to **Roger Bruce**, that would provide the necessary new material for the band to perform. Skiffle sold out as fast as it came in and Mo rolled with the flow. **Wilf Clare** was recruited to provide bass, a rarity in 1957. Acoustic guitars were exchanged for electric models that could be amplified, and after a few rehearsals, in came **Brian Sharpe**, from the **Houn'dogs**, com-plete with his full kit of drums and with **Dave Roberts** as the good looking boy up front, the Noisy Boys became the **Rockin' Modernaires**.

The Modernaires' first rehearsal at the Custard House, Bordesley Green

The emergence of the Mods, as they were often known, coincided with a visit to Birmingham by **Mel Lees** who was working for a Wolverhampton company - **Cliff and Halifax**. The company had opened a ballroom, the **Dorchester**, in Wolverhampton, and Mel's brief was to visit the **West End Ballroom** in Birmingham and steal a few ideas. What Mel saw on arrival at the West End was the Mods auditioning for the chance of a booking. Immediately Mel offered them the engagement at the Dorchester. They accepted it there and then, and subsequently proved a terrific success with the Black Country audiences. The Mods had now been augmented by **Maurice 'Moss' Groves**, a Yardley lad, who played quite superb saxophone and with **Tom Russell** from Green Lane, Small Heath on guitar, they were a great rock, 'n' roll combo and what is more, they were on the road! Mel Lees would chauffeur the vocalist, Dave, in his Ford Consul, Mo would cram the amplifiers into the tiny Jowett bread van that he'd bought from Wimbush's and Brian Sharpe would have his drums and the rest of the band tucked into his ultra flash Ford Farnham estate car.

The Vikings at the Wolseley Club, 1958

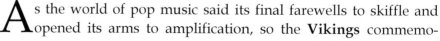

As the world of pop music said its final farewells to skiffle and opened its arms to amplification, so the **Vikings** commemorated the event by making a professional recording of their work at the **Hollick and Taylor** studio in Grosvenor Road, Handsworth where they cut 'Streamline Train' and 'Gambling Man'. From then on it was electricity all the way with **George 'Duke' Mann** playing guitar and handling the vo-

cals, **Terry Wallace** and **Paul Evans** also on guitars, **Johnny Jolly** on bass, **Mick Cope** from the **Rainbow Boys** on slide and **Alan Compton** on drums. Pubs such as the **Swan** in Washwood Heath and clubs like the **Wolseley** in Drews Lane were regular haunts for the Vikings as was the **Blakenhale** youth club, which was fast becoming the place to play for every ambitious band, even though it had no drinks licence, and therefore only pop to quench the thirsts of mean looking Teddy Boys.

The Vikings at the Swan, Washwood Heath 1958

Birmingham was becoming 'alive to the jive'. At the **Colisseum**, in Bearwood, the **Deltas** would be in attendance. At the Regan's new **Plaza**, Handsworth, it was **Tex Detheridge and the Nashvilles**, a band that had a couple of 'Rookery Roaders' in its line up, **Derek Bevins** and **Rue Shirley**. The **Nelson** pub in Ladywood had that wonderful outfit the **Tiger Sharks**, with **Harry Belcher** and Rex now being joined by guitarist **Tony Elson** with **Chick Bennett** on drums. The Tiger Sharks entered, and won, a beat group contest at **Birming-**

The Tiger Sharks at the Nelson, Ladywood

ham **Town Hall** in February '58. The contest was judged on audience reaction and so **George Bennett**, their manager, arranged for the staff, drivers and conductresses from Acocks Green bus garage to scream and invade the stage as the Tiger Sharks performed. Uproar followed the judges' decision to proclaim the Sharks as winners, because the favourites had been the **Rocking Tuxedoes**, led by pianist **Mick Pinder**. Mick wasn't too happy about being eclipsed by the Sharks, but he had the last laugh when six years later he became a founder of the legendary **Moody Blues**.

O ver in Sparkhill, at **St Ivor's Church Hall**, every Tuesday evening, the **Grasshoppers** would rock the joint. They'd begun as Tony's skiffle band at **Shirley Carnival** two years previously but had made rapid progress with regard to their ability as a result of enthusiastic practice sessions above **Wheatley's** joinery shop in Golden Hillock Road. Most Tuesday evenings, in the crowd, would be a few girls from Tyseley. One girl from this crowd nursed a secret ambition to 'have a go' with the band. **Brenda Bosworth**, from Sunningdale Road was that young lady. As she sipped her orangeade one particular Sunday evening in early '58, she thought she was hearing things. The band were calling out her name. Obviously, one of her friends had betrayed her secret wish. This was it! No turning back! Brenda took the microphone and hollered out the song 'Lollipop', which at the time was high in the charts by a British vocal trio, the **Mudlarks**. Brenda's 'bluesy' voice coming out of a petite frame that oozed charisma was an absolute knockout that night. So much so that **Brian Newman**, who had begun playing snare drum for the band but now managed them, offered her the vocalist job there and then, setting Brenda immediately on a path that was to earn her the title of Brum's 'Little Miss Dynamite.'

Little Miss Dynamite – Brenda Bosworth – with Grasshopper Dave Carter

T he **Rollercoasters** were no more. **Pete Worrall** rounded up some pals, **Alan Oldacre**, **Larry Sheil**, **Tom Williams** and **Eric Foxall**, switched to 'electric' and taking the name **Danny Burns**, his band became the **Phantoms**. With 'the bumbly wagon,' as they called it, for transport, they appeared at the **BRS Club** and the **Aston Chain and Hook**

Social, on the Bromford Lane leg of their grand tour of Erdington. Life wasn't all roses though for Danny and his Phantoms. On arrival at the **Erdington YMCA** on Reservoir Road, they found the stage guarded by wire mesh because the Kingstanding teddy boys had a habit of pelting the bands with anything they could lay their hands on!

Danny Burns & the Phantoms

Another 'school' skiffle outfit was the **Thunderclaps**. First seeing the light of day at Stirchley School, **Dennis Ryland**, from Ivy Road, Stirchley, and **Mal Strawford** from Beaumont Road, Bournville had commenced their working lives at Cadburys. Encouraged by the blind **Walter Thornton** to paticipate in social events, the Thunderclaps appeared at the annual Grand Concert in the **Cadbury Theatre**, along with another bunch of Cadbury workers, the **Wildcats**, featuring **Grant Harvey** and **Mark Raymond**.

Exactly what the Cadbury family, who are strict Quakers, thought about their young male employees singing songs that told of all night sessions with 'Miss Molly at the house of blue lights,' we can only imagine, but the audience loved every minute, including Walter Thornton!

"All the workers in the audience knew me as **Ken Hoban** from Dawlish Road!" laughed Mark, "But I dreamed up this fancy name, **Mark Raymond**. I got Mark from Marks and Sparks and Raymond from that hairdresser bloke, Mr Teezy Weezy!"

Wildcats at the Station, Selly Oak

Mal Strawford's father, on seeing his lad's band whip up a storm immediately arranged an engagement at the **Ladywood Social Club** for fifteen bob a-piece.

Tony Elson, at this time, had to say farewell to the **Tiger Sharks** because the band had become so popular that they were performing almost every evening. Tony, being an apprentice baker at Kunzle's, had to be at the ovens by five-thirty. He didn't have any transport and travelled everywhere by bus.

"One night," explains his mother, **Josie Elson**, "with his guitar tucked under his arm, travelling on the night service up Pershore Road, he meant to alight at the Dogpool pub. Sadly, he fell asleep with exhaustion and woke at the Man in the Moon, West Heath. Stumbling off the bus and semi-conscious, he didn't know where he was. He must have been guided back to Highbury by the stars above!"

It wasn't, however, goodbye to music and all the fun that went with it. Sunday lunchtimes would see Tony and his pals in the back room of the **Highbury** pub, playing for the sheer enjoyment of making music. They were just lads, barely out of school, yet sharing a love for the famous three or, by now, even four chords. Pals like **Dennis Ryland**, **Mal Strawford** and a youngster from the prefabs just over from the pub, a cheeky but loveable character, **Johnny Carroll**, who had the 'gift of the gab' and a gag for every occasion. There was **Mick Pinder** from Wheelwright Road, Erdington and a lad from Holcombe

Danny King & the Dukes at Butlins, Ayr

Road, Tyseley - **Brian Hines** - who even then, as a sixteen year old, was having difficulty in hiding his burning ambition to be up there where he would eventually belong. But in that summer of '58, the hit parade was light years away.

The warm summer air did bring success to **Danny King and the Dukes** though. The boys were already showing class and this was spotted by Butlins' talent scouts who signed them for the gig of a lifetime - a season at their Ayr Holiday Centre on the Scottish West Coast. Here they were paid a regular wage, fed correctly at meal times and provided with chalets. All they had to do was to 'rock the joint' six nights a week. It was 'cake' for these Summer Lane kids, who even then, were hardened professionals.

Independent Television had launched a show to rival BBC's Six-Five Special. Oh Boy! produced by Jack Goode and presented alternately by Jimmy Henney and Tony Hall, was to be the show that gave Cliff Richard his big break, and his first recording, 'Move It', the exposure a commercial record needs to 'chart.' This was the inspiration that **Mike Tyler** had been waiting for. As he sat in his mother's prefab on Druids Heath, watching Mr Richard going through his paces, he realised that this was the career for him. It was what he'd dreamed of during those sleepy afternoons at Hope Street and Wheelers Lane schools. On leaving school, Mike 'went on the milk,' but he'd begun to teach himself piano and could actually play the famous three chords in any key! This acquired skill had opened the show-biz door for him when he became the pub piano player at the **Maypole** pub, Warstock. A man honest with himself, Mike knew he had the looks and the voice. All he needed was a band.

Assembling together the finest creative talent in Druids Heath, over the course of a few weeks, he put them through their musical paces in a shed on nearby allotments. He even dreamed up a name. Calling himself **Cliff Britton**, after his new-found hero, he named the band the **Crusaders**. Sadly, the band didn't work out, although Mike continued honky-tonking in the Maypole bar. A regular 'free and easy' singer at the Maypole was Vince, an Elvis sound-alike from Highters Heath. Vince asked Mike to have 'I Go Ape' ready and rehearsed up for the following Saturday evening as Vince intended to bring Warstock to a halt with his delivery of the Neil Sedaka hit. Realising that a minor chord was in the arrangement, Mike spent all week practising the piece. Come Saturday evening and no Vince! But like a true professional, Mike did the song, milking as only a milkman can, everything from his performance. The crowd were ecstatic. The bar was in uproar. As far as they were concerned, a star was born. Watching the performance, through the haze of the Woodbine fumes, was **Cyril Viles**, from Fox Hollies. Cyril was well known to the local scene, finding engagements for bands and helping out with transport. When Mike took his break, Cyril introduced himself. Did Mike wish to join a proper band? A band that was rapidly making a name for itself as **Billy King and the Nightriders**? "Yes please," said Mike, although he could only play with them when the venue had a piano in its function room. One thing was certain. Mike's good looks would not be overlooked for long. When Billy King announced his retirement from performing, Mike was promoted to become the front-man of the Nightriders. He needed a stage name. Having recently seen the film Genaveve, he'd fallen in love with Anne Sheridan. That was it! Sheridan! **Mike Sheridan and the Nightriders**! Billy King became restless. He was missing the limelight and the female adoration after just a few days. He told the boys that Mike was to be ousted and he re-instated. Sadly for Billy King, the Nightriders (who were, at that time, drummer **Roger Spencer**, late of **Johnny Neal's Houn'dogs**; guitarists **Dave Pritchard** and **Max 'the Nub' Griffiths**, so called because of the permanent presence of a Woodbine nub hanging from his bottom lip, even when singing at the microphone, and **Brian Cope** on bass) were having none of it. Mike Sheridan remained.

Like Mike Sheridan, **Johnny Carroll** was educated at Hope Street School, Balsall Heath where he proudly maintains that he learned the values of respect and good manners. Following the sad event of his father's death, Johnny moved, at the age of ten, with his mother up to Highbury. In 1958, encouraged by his pal **Tony Elson**, Johnny bought a Framus sunburst guitar 'on the drip' from **Woodroffe's** for sixteen pounds. Taking lessons from Tony, he would practice until his fingers sometimes bled and Tony's mother, Josie, still laughs today at the memories of Tony and Johnny playing Buddy Holly's 'Maybe Baby' so loudly through an amplifier that was aimed out of Tony's bedroom window to broadcast their efforts over 'leafy' Highbury Park. Sometimes, on a Saturday evening, in the summer of '58, Johnny and Tony would cross Pershore Road, and amble up Umberslade Road, to **Muntz Park** where, if the weather was fine, jive dances would be held that featured **Danny Ray and the**

Mike Sheridan & the Nightriders with Joe Brown

Danny Ray & the Rave Ons play Muntz Park as fans bop in the open air

Rave Ons, 'Danny' being **Ray Humphries**, formerly a **Nignog**, as was guitarist **Bob Bradley**.The pair were joined by drummer **Colin Fortnam, Malc Hamilton** and saxist **Mick Biddle**.

"Muntz Park was big deal for us," stated Ray, "They had a house Tannoy system with speakers perched up in the surrounding beech trees, oh yeah, and fairy lights in the trees as well. We only had one amplifier and so we put the house mic in front of it. After the first spot the 'parkie' pleaded with us to turn down as complaints about babies being woken in their cots were coming in from Highbury, a mile away!"

Johnny Carroll, **Tony Elson** and **Dennis Ryland** needed a drummer and they let their needs be known to **Cyril Viles**. If he couldn't find them a drummer, then no one could. As it happened, Cyril, a keen table tennis player, used to play his ping-pong at Hall Green YMCA, where he would sometimes put himself up against a promising youngster, **Tim Bellamy**, from Arnold Grove, Shirley. After one such game, the conversation turned to the local music scene and Cyril mentioned his involvement in it. Tim let it be known that he was indeed a drummer of some standing, and, by coincidence knew **Brian Hines** vaguely because Brian was dating a girl from Arnold Grove, where most nights Brian would arrive on his Vespa scooter and whisk her off to a local hop.

Cyril wasted no time in placing Tim with the Highbury lads who were now called the **Dakotas**. A booking for them at the **Selly Park Legion Club** brought the boys into contact with local character **Joe**

Maltese Joe keeps an eye on the Dakotas at Cannon Hill Park

Cusheri, known to his associates as **Maltese Joe**. Joe became manager, head cook and bottle-washer for the Dakotas. His daytime activity was that of a mobile fruit and veg man. He would load up his Volkswagen van and 'work the knocker' until lunchtime when he would park up on the front of the Legion club on Pershore Road, and sell his leftover stock.

Sometimes however, the stock would remain unsold and Johnny, Dennis, Tony and Tim would be forced to travel to the evening's engagement sitting on sacks of spuds and cabbages as they made their way to the **Ariel** at Bournbrook, where **Cyril Viles** worked, or up the road to the **Taboo Club**, which was the church hall on Hazelwell Lane, facing Bournville Baths and where **Tom Withey** from Ivy Road promoted the evening's dance session, being 'assisted' by **Ray Romad**, the half Arab, half Welshman whose speciality in life was escorting unruly gents from the premises.

The **Six-Five Special** was back in town, but this time as a talent contest for bands at the **Gaumont Cinema**. Young hopefuls from all over Birmingham turned up to participate in this extravaganza. From Erdington came **Danny Burns and the Phantoms**, parking their 'bumbly wagon' in Weaman Street, and from Highbury came the **Dakotas**, emerging from the back of **Maltese Joe**'s fruit and veg van and into the glare of the Gaumont foyer. They were brimming with confidence. **Tony Elson** and **Johnny Carroll** were convinced that the hours of practice on their 'Guitar Boogie Shuffle' routine would place them in front of every other band. As well as that they planned to premier their 'Everlys' style of singing that evening. On entering the auditorium, however, their faces dropped as the ultra polished **Deltas** whizzed through 'Guitar Boogie' at break-neck speed, *plus,* the Deltas had matching red suits and crocodile shoes, shiny guitars and amplifiers that easily handled the vastness of Birmingham's most prestigious cinema. As the Dakotas took the stage, nerves were telling on Johnny's face, a face that normally oozed confidence. He pleaded to Tony, "Go on, you start!" but the house mic, being 'open' amplified his plea around the Gaumont. The audience rocked with laughter as the two lads hurled themselves into 'Bye Bye Love.'

It was bye bye **Gaumont** for the **Dakotas** as the **Deltas** made off with the trophy, but the Dakotas weren't disheartened. As he clambered back over the sprout bags and sacks of spuds in Maltese Joe's wagon, **Johnny Carroll** knew that one day, folks would take notice of him and see him for what he was, the most natural and comical of entertainers.

The Gaumont Cinema
Steelhouse Lane

Pat Wayne and **Johnny Neal** were now being recognised as singers with possibilities and their efforts were rewarded when ATV's Reg Watson and Kit Plant invited Pat and Johnny to guest on a pre Christmas television show, 'Roll Back the Carpet', to be transmitted from the Aston studios. That evening Pat and Johnny gave their all into the impersonal cameras, wiggling their hips as they sent the mainly female studio audience into a frenzy. Johnny Neal hollering out Elvis' 'Let's Have a Party' and Pat doing Paul Anka's 'Diana'. Pat, however, was not a happy man. Emerging onto Aston Cross, he felt that a more ambitious approach to his professional future would be beneficial to him. After the transmission, as he sauntered along Aston Road North that damp, smoggy December evening, Pat bought a copy of the Birmingham Mail and sought shelter in the appropriately named **Last Chance Cafe**. After purchasing a mug of Camp coffee and a Wagon Wheel from proprietor **John Butler**, known to his customers as *JB*, Pat began scanning the 'sits vac' column in the newspaper. Seeing an advertisement for Co-Op milkmen, he telephoned the following morning and arranged an interview. On arrival at the High Street store, he was directed to the personnel department on a higher floor. He failed to notice, as he ambled through the shoe department, that the female assistants were ceasing duties to stare at him. Suddenly it happened. One girl made the first move and grabbed him. Others quickly followed, screaming "It's him! It's him!" mobbing him, trying to pull the red and black drape jacket off his back. The commotion was eventually brought to a halt by a 'Molly Sugden' type middle aged lady clapping her hands and shouting for order.

"Who are you and what do you want?" she screamed.

"I've come about the milkman's job," answered Pat, struggling to break free of the female mob, patting his black Brylcreamed hair back into place as he did so. He'd failed to realise the power of television and the impact his appearance had made. He also failed to meet the requirements of the Co-Op's personnel department.

Chapter Five

YOU SHAKE MY NERVES

Football took preference to rock 'n' roll in **Micky Bakewell's** world back in '58. He'd excelled at soccer whilst attending Cockshut Hill School in South Yardley and, on leaving and commencing as an apprentice at Rover, Solihull, he was invited to play for Birmingham City Football Club's youth team by its famous talent scout, **Don Dorman**, on condition that Micky trained at St Andrew's every Tuesday and Thursday evening. This arrangement worked well for a while and a few bob from the 'Blues' came in handy to the lad who was handing over his wage packet to his widowed mother. However, the magic of rock 'n' roll moves in mysterious ways and Micky discovered that not only could he strum a guitar, he also had a voice. So, be it for the cause of rock 'n' roll or the chance to pull a few birds, Micky Bakewell, found himself with the difficult task of replacing the 'Marty Wilde of the Midlands' — **Billy Wakeham**. As a new member of the **Grasshoppers**, alongside **Dave Carter**, **Keith Adams** and **Tony Finnister,** he shared vocals with **Brenda Bosworth**.

"Without realising what was happening, the music took the place of football," says Micky. "If the band had a gig, I'd do the gig and skip training."

They would travel, in the luxury of a Hillman Utility truck with a canvas back, to gigs like the **Staffordshire Volunteer**, Wolverhampton, **Brierley Hill Town Hall** and the **Drill Hall, Coventry** as well as every Sunday at **Blakenhale Schools**, sharing the bill with either the **Stan White** or the **Viv Jones** bands. The Grasshoppers had built up a strong following and with the bonus of 'a few extra bob' to give to his mother, things were looking good for Micky.

Things were also looking good for **Danny King and the Dukes**. On returning home from their summer season in Ayr, they found themselves appearing at the **Aston Hippodrome** as part of the **Pauline Penny Revue** for a whole week! The compere for this extravaganza was a certain **Larry Grayson** and as Larry announced the band, so into the spotlight would step Danny (now sporting dyed blonde hair), the **Hancox** brothers and **Clint Warwick**, local lads from 'The Lane', blowing away the cobwebs of Aston's famous auditorium with such gems as 'Sea Cruise' and Danny's mum's favourite, Charlie Gracie's 'Fabulous'.

The mid '60s would see Britain swept away on the tide with the California sound of the Beach Boys singing songs of California girls being the most beautiful creatures on God's earth. However, six years earlier, in '58, the California sound was spearheaded by **Jimmy Holden**, **Mick Burrows**, **Roy Bates** and **Colin Smith**, collectively known as the **Dominettes**. We're talking, of course, about the region that separates Harborne from Weoley Castle. In those days the **California**, a magnificent pub named after its location, stood proudly on Barnes Hill, at the junction with Alwood Road. Here the Dominettes were joined by bassist **John Husthwaite**, whose brother Dave was in the Deltas, and guitarist **Bob Burlison**. They used their residency at the pub to launch their very own style of raw rhythm and blues.

The Ramrods at St Margaret's Church Hall and with Keith Powell at Aston Chain & Hook Club

As it became apparent that rock 'n' roll was here to stay, **Keith Powell** made the transition from the **Ernie Lane Dance Band** to the more raunchy **Ramrods**. With guitarist **Al Hawkins**, (who, incidentally, performed 'jive' demonstrations with his wife Edie around the ballrooms of Birmingham), Keith Powell and the Ramrods set out to ride the trail. That trail would take them to the **Bordesley YMCA**, **Aston Chain and Hook Club** and **St Margaret's Church Hall** at Washwood Heath, where the young females were swept off their feet by the young male singer with his Mediterranean looks and husky, bluesy voice.

The **Vikings**, at this time were forced to make changes. **'Duke' Mann**, who handled the vocals, was doing his National Service and only home at weekends. Whether it was the need to fulfil his patriotic duty or a couple of Military Police marching him up Washwood Heath Road we shall never know, but he resigned his post with the Vikings to be replaced by **Robert Hughes**, who rejoiced in the stage name of **Bobby Valentine**. With the Shadows now the darlings of British pop, the Vikings' other new recruit was

Duke's younger brother, **Johnny Mann** - an accomplished guitarist with the Hank Marvin touch.

Personnel changes were also happening with the **Deltas**. **Ray Vaughan**, the drummer, decided to emigrate. The guitarist, **Dave Husthwaite**, decided to join the merchant navy. Together, aboard Arcadia, they sailed to Australia, one as a passenger, the other as a steward. Both were quickly replaced. Guitarist **Eddie Maddox** was recruited, although Pat was feeling the need for a 'meatier' sound. What he needed was a keyboard player and if he'd become a Co-op milkman, he may never have found one.

Mal Strawford, or **Mal Ford** as he was now known, had become quite a celebrity at Cadburys, where he worked. A television show, **Sing-along with Joe**, a kind of visual 'Workers Playtime' featuring Joe 'Mr Piano' Henderson, had been broadcast from the Bournville factory and Mal, accompanying himself on piano, performed 'Livin' Doll' to the nation.

A week or so after his television debut he happened to visit the **Colisseum** at Bearwood, where he was so taken with the band, the Deltas, that he stayed late, missed the last bus and had to walk home. However, a few days later, he was at work, checking deliveries at the Cadbury gate, when a van from Atkins, the saw doctors of Bradford Street, pulled up. It was the usual delivery driver but Mal was surprised to recognise him as the singer from the Colisseum, **Pat Wayne**. Unfortunately Pat didn't recognise him from the television show, but when Mal introduced himself as a pianist, Pat agreed to audition him

Pat Wayne & the Deltas at Penns Hall, Sutton Coldfield

at the Oratory the following Sunday. By Monday Mal had joined the **Deltas** and recalls one appearance with the boys at **Penns Hall**, Sutton Coldfield. "The Deltas shared the billing with local lads from Sutton, **Johnny Whitehouse and the Congressmen**, who were announced as *direct from a tour of the Potteries!*"

It seemed that the Modernaires could

do no wrong. They were the talk of the town in Wolverhampton due to their success at the **Dorchester** and followed that by regular appearances at the town's **Scala Cinema**. **Mel Lees** was now heavily involved in the running of the Mods, who by now had taken to wearing stage attire from **Chetwyn's**, Navigation Street where big **Bill Lewis** saw to their every need. **Brenda Bennett**, the manageress of the Scala, noticed a piece in the Birmingham Mail announcing a grand beat group contest at the **Casino Ballroom**, Corporation Street. Not one to let the grass grow under his feet, Mel Lees quickly filled in the entry form. So did **Brian Newman**, manager of the **Grasshoppers**. There had to be a showdown sometime and this seemed a good a time as any.

"If the Grasshoppers had made use of their vocal ability, meaning Brenda Bosworth and me," recalls **Micky Bakewell**, "we'd have beat the Mods hands down." However, despite **Tony Finister** doing a brilliant drum solo on Cozy Cole's 'Topsy Part 2', the judges awarded in favour of the Modernaires, with **Gerry Day**, a great rocker, in third place.

Still, life goes on, the Grasshoppers took consolation by winning the Worcester beat group contest, held at the city's racecourse, and Mel Lees traded on the Casino success by securing engagements for the Mods at the **Firebird** in Carrs Lane and the **Swan at Yardley** which would eventually become a 'big gig' for the Modernaires.

For a band looking for snappy outfits, Chetwyns, Navigation Street, was a firm favourite

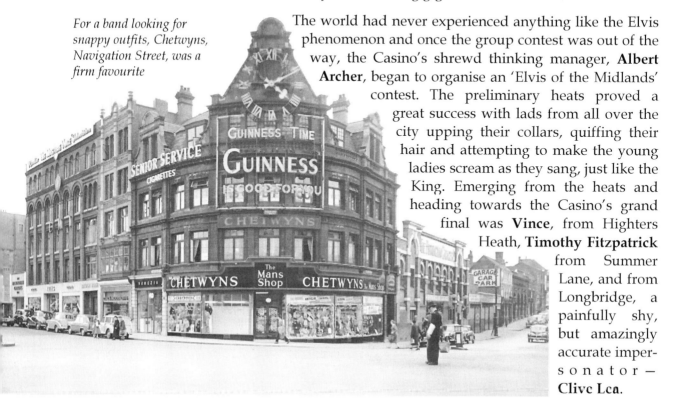

The world had never experienced anything like the Elvis phenomenon and once the group contest was out of the way, the Casino's shrewd thinking manager, **Albert Archer**, began to organise an 'Elvis of the Midlands' contest. The preliminary heats proved a great success with lads from all over the city upping their collars, quiffing their hair and attempting to make the young ladies scream as they sang, just like the King. Emerging from the heats and heading towards the Casino's grand final was **Vince**, from Highters Heath, **Timothy Fitzpatrick** from Summer Lane, and from Longbridge, a painfully shy, but amazingly accurate impersonator — **Clive Lea**.

The Waseley Hills, on the outskirts of Rubery, is where the River Rea rises. In 1956, Waseley Schools gave birth to the **Moonshine** skiffle group, led by guitarist **Pete Knight**. A couple of years on and Pete, like other Rubery lads, was a regular at Colmores Farm youth club where he met up with the Elvis finalist — Clive Lea. Together they hit on a formula that would secure the title. Pete would provide a backup band, just like Elvis's, to support Clive. The idea worked like a charm as Pete, **Mick Peplow**, **Mick Partridge** and **Dennis Ryland** gave the necessary 'umph' to Clive's version of the King's 'Paralysed'. Clive was awarded first prize, which was an appearance on **Lunchbox** performing the said song. Both he and the band also received a shoeshine kit each! Whether or not the lads took this as a hint to their appearance is another story but shortly afterwards they presented themselves at **Zissmans**, Bull Street as **Clive Lea and the Phantoms**, where Clive purchased a pink jacket and black shirt, and, for the band, powder blue suits at the cost of fourteen guineas each, which included in the price, two fittings.

Modernaires at the Swan, Yardley

At St Andrews football ground, **Micky Bakewell**'s constant absenteeism from training sessions had been noted by **Don Dorman**. Don pointed out that selection for the youth team could only be made if training commitments were honoured. Micky chose rock 'n' roll and headed off to meet with the **Grasshoppers** at the **Sydenham** pub on

Clive Lea & the Phantoms at the Wychbold Hotel, Sutton Coldfield

Golden Hillock Road, where at the age of seventeen he wasn't old enough to be on the premises, never mind singing in the band!

Above Dale Forty furnishings, on Erdington High Street was the **Carlton** ballroom and in the early to mid fifties dances were put on, as they were at the **Plaza**, Stockland Green and **Kyrle Hall**, Aston, by a gentleman by the name of Phillips.

Phillips Dances as they were known, would feature the music of **Fred Hobson** and **Norman**

The Carlton Ballroom, High Street, Erdington

Minnel, but it became apparent that their output was far too 'square'. Initially Danny King, the Dakotas, Danny Burns and such were recruited to play alternate sets with the 'pukka' band, but with dancers demanding more and more rock and no more 'hokey cokey' stuff, the way forward for the Carlton was clear. Having said that, who could have visualised back in '58, that nine years later, as a result of the 'Summer of Love', the Carlton would become one of the countries most important venues for its presentation of progressive music as **Mothers** club.

The **Apollo**, Tyburn Road, Erdington, began to present the **Saints and Sinners**, a trio, in between the 'Pearl and Dean' and the main film. **Micky Brassington** and **Brian Betteridge** played guitars whilst **Ray Thomas**, an apprenticed engineer at George Hughes Ltd of Erdington, would sing and occasionally blow on a harmonica. Eventually Brian and Ray began to plan the formation of a 'real' group. A drummer, **Ricky Wade**, was recruited, as was **John Lodge**, a guitarist who was apprenticed as a draughtsman at Parkinson Cowan. Calling themselves **El Riot and the Rebels**, they spent every available minute rehearsing in a hut on Marshbrook Road until the lads were satisfied that they were good enough to face an audience, which they did, at the **Birlec** club in Cheston Road, Aston, where John's father worked.

Christine Perfect – from fried onions to big Mac

On the other side of the City, **Brian Botfield** was busy making plans. He'd begun his secondary education at Turves Green School, where he discovered the joy of playing music by dabbling on clarinet, along with another pupil, **Geoff Turton**. On being accepted into Moseley Art School he found, to his dismay, no formal musical education available. There was however, an after school skiffle class run by a teacher, **Butch Baker**. The problem was though, how to play skiffle on a 'liquorice stick'. The answer? Buy a guitar, or in Brian's case, make one from a kit. Eventually, he bought the real McCoy and found his classical background on clarinet invaluable as he began to develop a bluesy technique on guitar. His pal at the Art School was a Buddy Holly look and sound alike from Erdington, guitarist **Bob Bates**. Soon they were augmented by a female student from the skiffle class who played piano. She was **Christine Perfect** from Bearwood, whose father, Cyril, was a professor at Birmingham University and her mother, Beatrice, a psychic and healer. Initially they were called the **Bobcats**, but not for long. Brian had been hearing Chuck

Berry records on the café juke box across from the Art School on Moseley Road. Thrilled by the sheer excitement of this rock 'n' roll poetry and blistering guitar style, their repertoire soon became well stocked with Chuck Berry material. Hence the name - the **Rockin' Berries**. And, because Brian could play exactly like the man from St Louis, he soon earned the nickname 'Chuck' for himself. Chuckling at the memory of their first gig, Brian recalls them being booked at the **Cofton Community Centre**, Groveley Lane, Longbridge, commonly known as the 'Gulley Club'. The Centre, unfortunately, had no piano for Christine to play, so, after searching around they came across **Bob Broomhall**, the hot dog man in Northfield, who not only loaned them his piano for the evening, he also transported it from his house to the Centre in his hot dog van. The evening was very successful, although Christine Perfect, who in later years was to be a member of that incredible creative force, **Fleetwood Mac**, did complain of the piano keys being sticky and smelling of fried onions!

Señor **El Riot** and his band of **Rebels**, in the meantime, were out riding the prairies of Pype Hayes, in search of places to play. Someone advised them to 'have a word with the gaffa at the Tyburn', which resulted in them taking up residence there every Monday evening where, for a fee of thirty shillings, **Ray Thomas**, alias El Riot, would take up a Gene Vincent stance and do 'Be bop a Lula' and 'Say Mama' whilst his amigo, **Brian Betteridge** would demonstrate his talent on guitar with such instrumentals as the appropriate 'Rebel Rouser' and the even more appropriate 'Tequila!'

Danny Burns & fans backstage at the Carlton Ballroom

The Deltas' Pat Wayne & Tony Butler at the Colisseum, Bearwood 1959

The
Swinging
"*Deltas*"
Rock
'N'
Twist
Combo

Electric Organ - Lead Guitar
Bass Guitar - Drums - Vocals

M. STRAWFORD,
67, BEAUMONT ROAD,
BOURNVILLE,
BIRMINGHAM, 30

The **Deltas**, in late '58, were spreading their wings as far as Kid-derminster. Every Friday evening would find them at **Frank Freeman's Ballroom**, where customers would bop away their blues to the 'big' sound that was coming from **Mal Ford's** Bird organ (like the one featured by Cherry Waynor on the 'Oh Boy' television show). After the gig, so drummer **Keith Seeley** recalls, they would head up the Hagley Road to Broad Street and the **Zambezi** coffee bar, still wearing their Lurex stage jackets, purely to show-off of course! However, the Lurex jackets offered little protection when the band appeared at the **Bournbrook**, Selly Oak.

"It always was a tough one," said **Pat Wayne**. "We'd just finished the last song of the first spot when a bunch of teds began pelting us with eggs. The eggs that missed us exploded on the back wall as we ran for cover."

Apparently, the gang had been evicted from the premises the week before but had managed to sneak back in the following week, although this time armed to the teeth with eggs for the band.

"Do you know," giggled Pat, "I was back at the Bournbrook in the early seventies and the stains on the wall were still there!"

Chapter Six

Gᴏᴛ SOME MONEY IN MY JEANS

Word had it that if you went to Upper Thomas Street School in Aston and had all of your teeth, you were a sissy. **Micky Gibbs** had a full set of molars but was no sissy. In fact he'd shown exceptional skills as a boxer, representing not only his school but also the Midlands ABA and was a member of the renowned Holte boxing club. However in 1959, at fifteen years of age, he realised that he had more chance with the ladies if he were to maintain his 'film star' looks and become a rock 'n' roll singer rather than a street corner lad with a pair of cauli-flower ears.

Seeking out two pals who could actually play their guitars, **Sprike Hopkins** and **John Watson**, he then managed to somehow find a drummer, **Alan Bennett**.

Evenings were spent in rehearsal until they mustered up courage to approach **Ken Smith**, who ran the **Say Mama** club, at **Maney Hall**, Sutton Coldfield and beg for an engagement. This was granted and Micky and the boys stood nervously on stage, awaiting Ken Smith's announcement.

"Ladies and gentlemen, boys and girls," he barked. "Would you please make welcome . . er . . . er . . . what's your name lads?"

"We haven't thought of one yet," answered Micky.

Quick as a flash Ken ad-libbed. He was a master showman. "Ladies and gentlemen, I give you **Cliff Angel and the Virtues!**"

The silence was deafening, but once the boys

Cliff Angel (nee Micky Gibbs) & the Virtues at Say Mama, Maney Hall, Sutton Coldfield

got into their stride, sanity returned to Maney Hall. After the interval Ken assured the boys that all was well. They were a good, rockin' outfit and he had the ideal name for them which he refused to divulge until, with microphone in hand, Ken announced, for the first of many times at Maney Hall and subsequently at many other of his promotions, "Ladies and gentlemen, let's hear it for **Gerry Levene and the Avengers**!"

Micky Gibbs' classmate from junior school days at Albert Road School was **Dezi Vyse**, who lived in Whitehead Road, Aston. Dezi fancied his chances as an accordionist, but being left handed, he couldn't get the hang of things, so he began to dabble on guitar with a few chords here and there. Unlike most other Aston lads, he would not be found on the terraces of Villa Park. Instead Dezi would spend his spare time at Birmingham Ice Rink, where he palled up with a lad from Camden Street by the name of **Peter Green**. By coincidence, Pete played a few chords on guitar, which he'd learned during a spell in hospital a year or so earlier at Blackwell, near Bromsgrove. One Autumn night in 1959, after witnessing Pete with his guitar, successfully serenading the local Spring Hill talent on the steps of the Ice Rink, Dezi decided to advertise his blades and put in with Pete Green.

Micky Gibbs alias Gerry Levene – molars intact

Rehearsals took place at either Micky or Pete's place, much to the annoyance of the neighbours. Pooling their savings, they invested in a second hand **Selmar** amplifier to bash their guitars through, and a microphone plugged into an old **Grundig** tape recorder would be suspended from the ceiling light to record their joint vocal efforts.

On leaving the army in early '59, **Paul Hewitt**, from Northfield, began working at the Austin Motor Works, Longbridge, where he met and befriended local character **Dougie Thompson**. Slightly older than Paul, Dougie could manage a few chords on guitar and had rock 'n' roll aspirations. Indeed, he had assembled a band with his brother-in-law, **Terry Bond** (a hospital clerk with a kit of drums) and another local lad, **Mark Johnson**, who also played a few chords. Dougie mentioned to Paul, as they worked away on the production line, that **Clive Lea and the Phantoms** were at the **Rubery Social Club** and it was his intention to poach Clive and have him in the group. On witnessing the performance that night, Paul casually said that Clive wasn't doing anything that he himself couldn't do. This was music to Dougie's ears as he hadn't fathomed out what he could possibly offer to the 'Elvis of the Midlands' that would tempt him from nice little earners with the Phantoms to total obscurity with the likes of Dougie Thompson! So Paul was taken at his word and put through his paces at **Hamstead Community Centre**, West Heath, where, after a stunning rendition of 'Livin' Doll', he was pronounced lead singer of — wait for it -- **Archimedes Deal**.

Everyone agreed that the name was awful. The **Rockin' Berries** was a far better name. Rockin' Berries? What's that got to do with the price of 'taters? Dougie Thompson *wanted* that name and only he could pull such a stroke. He'd heard of the Berries' young guitarist who played stunning licks in the Chuck Berry style. He also heard that they were about to disband but were playing a final gig at **Cotteridge School Hall**. Dougie offered **Brian 'Chuck' Botfield** a position with Archimedes Deal that night. Chuck agreed, but only on condition that they change their name — to the 'Rockin' Berries.' Dougie, after considerable thought, finally agreed!

Rockin' Berries at the George, Northfield with Chuck Botfield (5'6'' including the beer crate)

Further on down the road (the Pershore Road in fact) **Johnny Carroll** was, as they say in show-biz, resting. He'd broken away from the **Dakotas** to sit quietly and contemplate his future. Meanwhile, pianist **Mick Pinder** temporarily helped them out and did a first class job with his renditions of Johnny Preston's 'Runnin' Bear', complete with Red Indian war dances and chants.

Finally, as the Dakotas became the **Chequers**, **Cyril Viles** found two new members to make up for Johnny Carroll's absence. **Tex Detheridge** would perform his cowboy songs and share the limelight with a handsome heart-throb by the name of **Tommy Steele**. **Mal Ford** recalls one Sunday evening at his parents' house in Beaumont Road, Bournville, when Cyril Viles arrived panic stricken. Mal was quickly ushered from the house into the sidecar that was fixed to Cyril's motor bike and told that he was urgently needed to play piano for Tommy Steele. Mal was so nervous. He was a fair player but no Liberace. His mind was racing faster than the sidecar wheels as he tried to remember arrangements for 'Little White Bull' and other songs that one would associate with the boy from Bermondsey. As he scrambled out of the sidecar he noticed they'd arrived at the **Horse and Jockey**, Wythall. Once inside, "There he was," said Mal, "Tommy Steele from Nechells. A Billy Fury look-alike with a pint, a Woodbine and a Brummie accent that would cut diamonds!" From then on Mr Steele was known as **Tommy Dallas**.

A visit to the **Odeon** cinema in early '59 gave young **Steve Gibbons**, of York Street, Harborne, quite a shock. As the adverts finished and the audience settled back for the main feature, so a band shuffled on and played a short but impressive set of rock-a-billy. The band was **Tommy Hawk and the Hatchets**, but Steve recognised the singer as **Sid Hawkes**, a former fellow pupil of Station Road Secondary School, Harborne.

"It was the first band I'd ever seen," said Steve, "and Sid, from school, with a black rose guitar, was up there doing just what I wanted to do." Fortunately Steve didn't have to wait too long. He had been in the Boys' Brigade, the 64th Harborne to be exact, and a fellow brigader, **Alan Cox**, was now working at Kalamazoo, Northfield with **Colin Smith** and **Mick Burrows** from the **Dominettes**. Colin, the singer, was leaving to join with **Jimmy Powell** and his band, the **Detours**. The Dominettes needed someone with a voice. "Next thing I know," says Steve, "I'm in Mick Burrows' front room in Ludstone Road, Weoley Castle, going through my paces, all my Presley stuff. I joined there and then and did the **California** on the Friday. It was great! I was an apprentice plumber in those days, so I figured I'd fix the joint by day, and rock the joint by night!"

Gerry Levene, (note the spelling, so as not to be confused with the furniture retailers, Levine) and his **Avengers** were now up and running, and going for it. **Alan Bennett**'s father had a van, so he was appointed chauffeur and general gofer. Everything was fine until Alan took a holiday. The Avengers found a lad to deputise on drums but initial performances were disasterous — **Graeme Edge**, from Coventry Road, Small Heath, was used to playing jazz and had little or no feel for what he would have described as 'bubblegum stuff.' However, after the first few gigs, the Avengers and Graeme came to terms with one another. It began to work well. A little too well for Alan, because when he returned from holiday, he found Graeme firmly installed on the drummer's stool. Without Alan Bennett, they were also without a van and driver, and for a while they had to make do with Corporation buses. Still, ambitions could not be suppressed. They needed, as all bands did by now, a bass player. An advertisement in the **Birmingham Mail** resulted in another former Boys' Brigader of the 64th – **Jimmy Onslow** from Park Hill Road, Harborne, making his presence known. Jimmy had been part of **Bobby Earl and the Counts**, from Warstock. 'Bobby' being **Reg Jones** (whose much younger little blonde haired cousin, **Chris 'Ace' Kefford**, would follow him everywhere). The Counts had started up at the **Stonehouse Gang** youth club, Harborne, where, for a shilling, kids could play darts and ping-pong while the Counts practised up the corner.

Eventually the band came good and progressed up War Lane to appear regularly at the **Junction** pub. Their drummer, Barry, worked for the Initial Towel Company and had bought one of the works vans, a Commer, which he then sold to Jimmy for twenty three pounds. When Jimmy arrived to audition for the Avengers, they

Bobby Earl & the Counts at the Bournbrook

weren't impressed by his pink Fender bass, or his ability to play and dance around exactly like Jet Harris of the Shadows. It was Jimmy's Commer van that secured the job!

Perhaps it was the fumes from Holden's paint factory, or the sweet smell of Hughes biscuits floating around Bordesley Green, but something was firing ambition in

Half way through the season and the Mods had a visit from three starry eyed Brummie rockers. **Steve Gibbons**, **Jim Holden** and **Roy Bates** had heard the tales that were filtering back to Brum about the Mods blowing Margate apart. "We couldn't keep away," laughs Steve at the memory. "We got down there and the Modernaires let us do a couple of numbers. Fantastic! It was all happening. We didn't have any money so we went potato picking. Anything to just be there."

"We'd fasten advertising boards to the roof rack on Brian's car," recalls **Mel Lees**, "and drive up and down the front every morning, shouting at the birds to come and have a jive tonight to the Modernaires! Every night we packed 'em in."

Also attracting the birds were the Berries. The Rockin' Berries, that is, with a repertoire that was now very heavily rhythm and blues influenced. With songs like 'You're Right, I'm Left, She's Gone' and 'Money Honey', a good boppin' night was guaranteed for all at **Culmington Hall**, Turves Green, and the **Co-Op Rooms**, Kings Norton Green.

Dougie Thompson was now working as a dray-man for Ansells, the brewers. He happened, one day, to be delivering to the **Palace** in Redditch. It had once been a theatre and later a dance hall but, apart from the upstairs club bar, it hadn't been used for ages. Always looking for a deal, Dougie arranged with the manager that if the Berries cleaned up the dance hall, they could 'take the door' themselves. The following Saturday, five would-be pop stars could be seen marching over Church Green East, Redditch, armed with buckets, brooms, mops and packets of Borax. Chuck, now working as a commercial artist, did the posters, and the Berries opened for business at the Palace a week later with a free matinee followed by an evening session that carried a half-crown entrance fee. Dougie Thompson, in his wisdom, thought it best to have the **Hoffman Twins** from West Heath, as friends rather than enemies and employed them as doormen. Within four weeks the place was full by seven o'clock.

El **Riot and the Rebels** were feeling pretty confident regarding their future. Up until now, **John Lodge** had played his rhythm guitar with the bass full up and the treble off to compensate the lack of a bass guitar, but now bass guitars were becoming readily available. On finding an excellent guitarist, **Micky Herd**, to play alongside **Brian Betteridge**, John invested in a proper bass and with the Rebels now sounding like a force to be reckoned with, they also took on board a saxophonist, a Scotsman, **'Little' Jimmy**. Sadly, the story takes a tearful twist here because, on his way to an engagement with the boys, Jimmy crashed his motorcycle outside the Clock Garage on the Chester Road and died as a result of his injuries. Although obviously deeply shocked, the boys had to continue down that rock 'n' roll highway. Spreading their wings somewhat, El Riot and his Rebels were beginning to travel south of the border down Bromsgrove way to the **Forest** pub, the **Longbridge** at Rubery and, homeward bound, they would fiesta at the **Navigation** at Bromford.

Peter Green and **Dezi Vyse**, ice skaters turned rockers, now had a repertoire of songs to perform to their public. But where was their public? Pete's uncle, **Phil Peters**, had the answer. A former ballroom dancer of some repute, Phil had influential contacts in and around the city. Consequently a telephone call was made to **Wally Tovey**, the entertainment secretary of **Shard End British Legion**. A date for the lads' show-biz debut was entered into the club's diary of forthcoming attractions. Phil Peters mentioned a fee but Wally Tovey was a humane and gentle man. "Money isn't everything," sighed Wally, slotting the dog-end of his Park Drive back behind his ear.

Pete and Dezi, for a while, became the darlings of Shard End British Legion, especially when the boys were accompanied by the house drummer, **Fred Allport**.

Modernaires' guests – Steve Gibbons, Jim Holden & Roy Bates at Margate Pier Ballroom

"I remember us doing 'Apache'," giggles Dezi Vyse. "Fred had this row of skulls fitted onto the front of his drum kit. As Pete and me swung our guitars up in the air, like the Shadows, so Fred would switch to drumming on the skulls. The sound of the skulls and the effect it had on the audience was incredible. Fred was way ahead of his time."

Someone knocking on the window of Mrs Carroll's prefab was about to bring her son, Johnny, back into the spotlight. It was **Roger Smith**, from Wellsford Road, Solihull. He had wandered into **Hobday's** record shop in Kings Heath and mentioned that he was in search of a guitarist to form a band with him and his wife, Audrey. Mr Hobday sent him straight round to see **Johnny Carroll**, and a new band soon kicked into life – the **Olympics**.

When they started rehearsals at the **Maypole** pub, **Ted Brown**, the licensee, spotted true potential. He also spotted a way to compete with **Mike Sheridan**, who, with the **Nightriders**, was now the regular attraction down the road at the **Shirley Annexe**. One night, as the Olympics went through their paces, Ted Brown set up shop and began charging a 1/6d entrance fee. Johnny revelled in the challenge and, not content simply to sing and play his guitar, he started putting a few 'funnies' into the show. After two weeks **Jimmy Murray**, the bouncer from the Ritz was placed on the door to keep out the 'riffraff' as word spread rapidly about this guitar playing, gag telling song and dance man. Yes, dance man! Johnny's party-piece was **Green Door**, and the Maypole would go wild as he kicked his leg high into the air, á la **Frankie Vaughan**.

Johnny Carroll by day

Johnny acquired a great prop for the act through his new day job as a dustman. "It happened in Grange Road, Kings Heath," he recalls. "As I came down an entry with a bin on my back, so a front door opened and a woman shouted "'Ere, stick this on the cart!" and threw something out onto the pavement. It was a top hat, just like Frankie Vaughan's." Johnny tried the hat for size. It fitted perfectly. "Thank you," he said to the heavens, brushing the bed fluff from the brim. The following week when Johnny did his high-kicking Green Door routine, he produced the top hat and, as he wobbled it about on his forehead, Warstock shook with the audience reaction. The disappointment of the Gaumont talent show was behind him. The future was all that mattered — and what a future Johnny Carroll had to look forward to. "I was never the greatest guitar player," he admitted, "I just got by with my personality."

It was a personality of which, one day, the whole nation would be aware.

Chapter Seven

DON'T FORGET WHO'S TAKING YOU HOME

With a few bands now enjoying the luxury of some sort of van, moving around from gig to gig became more pleasurable to the point where the musicians, after their performances, would look for a place to unwind. Sited at the back of the Crown, Hill Street, on the corner of Hinckley Street, stood a catering caravan that served hot dogs with onions at ten pence. Meat pies (soft bottomed, of course) were one shilling, eight pence for steak and kidney, two shillings for chicken and mushroom, and a thrupenny bit would buy you a cup of tea. With such value, Alex Douglas's **Snackerie**, or as it was more commonly known, **Alex's Pie Stand,** soon became the late night rendezvous for Birmingham's rock 'n' roll musicians. As the pub and cinema clientele began to disperse from around the pie stand to their various late night bus services, so the bandwagons, containing half starved musicians, still on a high from their performances, would start parking up in Hinckley Street. Indeed **Keith Powell** recalls that the drummer with the **Jaymen, Jimmy White** from

Alex's Pie Stand — the Snackerie

Ladywood, would arrive at the pie stand every night and demolish three pies in one session! Burning their lips and tongues, more often than not, on the piping hot gravy and boiling tea, the musicians would share in gossip about the local scene. It was all riveting stuff to young men, some just out of school but all sharing one cause, the rock 'n' roll dream.

Brian Hines from Tyseley shared that dream. Pat Wayne recalls meeting Brian at the pie stand. "Brian wasn't in a band, but he was always on the look-

out for some experience. The **Deltas** needed a bass player for a few weeks and he jumped at the chance. We used to rehearse at the **Billesley Community Centre** then. He was just so determined to make it. Brian never travelled with us in our wagon. He went everywhere on his Vespa scooter with his bass guitar strapped to the back of the saddle. Of course, I'd do most of the singing, but when Brian did a song, every word of the lyric hit home."

Johnny Dean & the Dominators at Shirley institute

As Pat Wayne said, it was to be only a short flirtation with the Deltas for Brian Hines. Opportunity came knocking for him when his drummer pal from Arnold Grove, **Tim Bellamy**, **Dave Wheeland** from Grove Road, Sparkhill, and **Tony Elson**, his mate from Sunday lunchtime bashes at the Highbury pub, decided that what Birmingham needed was *another* group. They even had a name for it. It was to be called the **Dominators**, after the Norton motorcycle, and the front man would be a fictitious character, **Johnny Dean**; in other words, Brian Hines. With **Cyril Viles** spending his time, firstly on the telephone to various promoters, informing them of the arrival of this superstar band, and then transporting them round in his Atlas van, Johnny Dean and the Dominators quickly became crowd pleasers at the **Mermaid**, Stratford Road and Sutton Coldfield's shrine to rock 'n' roll, the **Say Mama**, **Maney Hall**, where, on hitting the last note of the last song of the set, Johnny Dean would demonstrate his gymnastic skills with backflips and cartwheels across the stage and the front of the dance area to the delight of the girls in the audience, although sometimes he'd receive menacing looks from their boyfriends, some of whom were the 'Kingstanding Teds' no less!

"Some of those teds scared the daylights out of **Clive Lea**," recalls **Pete 'Hank B' Knight** of the **Phantoms**. "Clive used to drive the girls wild at the Say Mama with his Elvis impressions, but he'd never let his eyes meet theirs. He was just so scared of the consequences."

This was not the case with **Gerry Levene and his Avengers**. Nothing frightened Gerry. He'd look the ladies right in the eyes and sing that immortal

Johnny Dean & the Dominators at the Crown & Cushion, Perry Barr

lyric 'One night with you is what I'm now praying for!' By day, Gerry, as Micky Gibbs, was working at his cousin's record shop, **Oldridge's**, in Selly Oak. A regular customer was a fellow who worked at the **West End Ballroom**, Suffolk Street, as lighting and sound man in the evenings and pot man in the mornings. He knew of Micky's musical activities and invited Gerry and the Avengers to audition at the West End on the following Sunday evening with a view to regular work there. Micky Gibbs could hardly contain his excitement as he and the lads arrived and began setting up on that hallowed stage, preparing to play for dancers to jive on that specially sprung floor. However, their excitement cooled when the resident musicians, **Fred Brinklow**'s band, arrived and told them to "'op it!" A very nervous Micky Gibbs approached the manager of the establishment, **Eric Lardner**, and pleaded his case. Although he knew nothing of the soundman-cum-potman's arrangements, Mr Lardner

West End Ballroom manager, Eric Lardner with Billie Davies & Keith Powell

allowed Gerry Levene and the Avengers to perform whilst Fred Brinklow and his musicians had a lie down.

As a result of their performance, an alliance between Gerry Levene and the West End Ballroom began, which would see the band performing there every Wednesday and Saturday lunchtime. It also gave the Avengers great publicity because Mecca, the proprietors, advertised heavily on

railway station platforms. "Everywhere you looked," said Micky, "you saw our name — *Gerry Levene and the Avengers at the West End*! Everything in big letters!"

Mike Sheridan and the Nightriders were also benefiting thanks to the Mecca organisation. The **Locarno** 1960 Beat Group Contest provided good publicity for all the groups that entered, but as the outright winners, Mike and his band took the lion's share.

Saltley's **Corsairs**, with a little juggling of personnel, became the **Andy Capps**. Original band members **Tommy Owen** and **Garth Quirke** brought in guitarist **Johnny Wileman** and drummer **Bob Sheward**. Tommy was now the proud owner of a Hofner guitar but, because he couldn't afford a case for it, his mother made him a velvet bag which he carried lovingly on the number 14 bus to gigs like the **BSA Tools Club** by the Mackadown, or the dance hall underneath the **Arcade Snooker Club** at Alum Rock. The Andy Capps *did* have vocalist, **Bob Buttery**, who was the bouncer from the Capital cinema, and it therefore followed that he was a feared man, but sadly, he was a better bouncer than a singer.

"None of us had the nerve to tell him what we thought of his voice, but one night Bob is testing the mic at the Arcade club," recalls Tommy. "One-two one-two and all that. This kid starts taking the mickey out of him. Suddenly Bob went for him. The kid ran out of the hall and Bob went after him. We never saw him again!"

Danny King & the Royals at the White Swan, Washwood Heath

Fortunately for the Andy Capps, **Danny King** was in the audience and filled in on vocals. Having recently split with the **Dukes**, who by now had **Gerry Day** singing for them, Danny needed a band. The Andy Capps fitted perfectly and offered no objection when Danny renamed them **Danny King and the Royals**. Bob Sheward explains how the name came about.

"The marketing people from Nestlé's Chocolate came to see us at the **Swan** in **Washwood Heath**. They had a product going, Royal Chocolate or something like that and they wanted Danny to promote it. So we became the Royals, and Danny

got chauffeured to certain engagements in a Roller!"

Born at the White Horse, Holborn Hill, Aston, where his parents kept the pub, **Greg Masters** moved, a few years later, with his folks, to the New Inns, on Great Lister Street, next to Pickfords. It was here that the young Greg developed his taste for melody.

"The licensing laws were strict in those days but dad used to put a singsong on in the back room on Sundays. I'd be upstairs in bed, listening to the great songs of the day by Frankie Laine and Johnny Ray, all that mob."

In '59 his parents moved out of the licensed trade to run a grocer's shop in Cato Street, Nechells, next to the dairy. Also living in Cato Street was a lad of the same age as Greg, **Johnny Killigrew**.

"Johnny had so much talent and enthusiasm for rock 'n' roll music," says Greg, "and taught me a thing or two on guitar. But he never really was in a group. He was in the **Tuxedos** with **Mick Pinder** for a while, but always seemed far too advanced in ability to stay around for long. We used to buy our records from the shop at the bottom of Cato Street, and Johnny eventually married Doreen, the girl who worked there."

Eventually, Greg Masters found himself a bunch of lads to form a band with. "I'd hang around **Yardleys** guitar shop, which was in the arches on Snow Hill. The young salesman, **Pete Oliver** (we used to call him 'Deadlegs') introduced me to **Roger Hill**, from Copeley Hill, off Slade Road in Erdington. His dad had the Hillfield Cycle Co, a few arches up from Yardleys. Roger and his brother **Bobby** worked for their dad, but Roger was never there! He was always in the guitar shop!"

The Evergreens

Greg, together with Roger and Bobby Hill, teamed up with bass player **Graham Gallery**, (whose father was something of a 'name' musician around Birmingham) and drummer **Vick Clarke**, to become **Bobby and the Dominators**.

From Boldmere School, on the border of Erdington and Sutton, came the **Evergreens**. Four lads, **Dave Cole**, **Nick Stevens** and **Ed Gateley**

Carl Fenn
& the Mysteries

played guitars whilst **Alan Buxton** thumped around on drums. "We all knew each other from school, and it started from there," said Alan. "Our first gig was at **Banners Gate Youth Club** for thirty bob, and we borrowed a barrow to cart our gear up the Chester Road."

The Evergreens became a regular feature around the youth club circuit and Alan recalls playing the **Streetley Youth Club**, where other regular faces would include **El Riot's Rebels** and another local outfit by the name of **Carl Fenn and the Mysteries**. The Mysteries - **Rob Nicholls**, **Don Hawkins**, **Carl Fenn**, **John Bradley** and **Ted Tunnicliffe** - had initially climbed aboard the rock 'n' roll carousel as the **Black Cats**, a school band at Bishop Vesey, Sutton Coldfield.

Expanding the line up to include **Martin 'Boots' Grice** and **Dean Forrester**, the Evergreens got kitted out with green suits from **Chetwyn's**. They finally made it to the 'big time' through appearances at the **Abbey Hall**, at the back of the church, across from the Lyndhurst estate.

"Somebody made a crack that we looked like Robin Hood's merry men," said Alan, recalling the first time they took to the stage wearing Lincoln green. Little did that heckler know that his casual comment would become fact within two years.

Bookings entered in the **Modernaires'** 1960 diary show just how much established bands were earning. On the 15th January the Mods appeared at **Haddon and Stokes** canteen in Digbeth, across from the Old Crown, for a fee of ten pounds. The following evening they were at **Blakenhale Schools** for six pounds, matched, the night after that by the **MEM Club** at Tyseley. The **Nautical Club** in Dean Street liked the cut of their jibs but could only manage three

THE (ROCKIN) MODERNAIRES

M. JONES,
80, BLAKE LANE,
BIRMINGHAM 9.

Phone:
VIC 2707

pounds. That blow, however, was cushioned when **Lonnie Donegan** turned up, out of the blue, and joined in with the fun. The **Sydenham**, on Golden Hillock Road, went for broke, paying them seven pounds and ten shillings; but the 'treacle on their pudding' came at the **Scala**, Wolverhampton, where they walked away with a cool fifteen quid!

The Modernaires meet Lonnie Donegan at the Nautical Club

Also coining the old 'sponduticks' were the **Rockin' Berries**, still packing them in at the venue that they had spruced up to run themselves — the **Palace**, Redditch. They could now afford to book guest bands into the venue and really give the punters value for money. **Danny King** and his new band, the **Royals** became regular faces, as did **El Riot and the Rebels**, now appearing in full Mexican bandit costumes, courtesy of Dunne's, Bull Street. Also making the odd appearance at the Palace, were **Clive Lea and the Phantoms**,

El Riot & the Rebels

with Clive now beginning to be noticed as an excellent impressionist.

"One minute he'd be Elvis, then Dick Emery. Popping on leather gloves and swinging his leg over the mic stand, he'd be Gene Vincent and then he'd do a hysterical Peter Sellers on 'Any Old Iron'," **Pete Knight** recalls.

With the **Rockin' Berries** becoming more and more ambitious, the name **Clive Lea** was once again figuring in **Dougie Thompson**'s thoughts and plans. The idea of having a record to play to prospective bookers appealed to the lads and so plans went ahead for them to record a demonstration disc at **Hollick and Taylor** studios in Handsworth. The Berries chose to record **Someday**, with singer **Paul Hewitt** doing a fair 'Ricky Nelson' on the vocal track.

The **Palace**, Redditch also played host to the **Dominettes** but things got a little out of hand half way through the evening, thanks to a visit by the notorious **Brookes Brothers**, the town's most feared teddy boys.

"I've never seen a fight like it," said **Steve Gibbons**, shaking his head but managing a chuckle. "As we were playing the Lonnie Donegan number 'San Miguel,' the whole dance floor erupted. There were blokes swallow-diving from the balcony into the fight. The band just ran for it but I got left behind. There was fighting on the car park, kicking and shoving out in the street. The band ran one way to the car but for some reason I ran the other and lost them. I had to walk home to Harborne!"

Modernaires at the Ritz, Kings Heath

The **Modernaires**, like the Berries, also joined the ranks of recording artistes at this time by putting down their party-pieces **Woodchoppers Ball** and **Tuxedo Junction** on **Status Records**, which was run by **Bill Huntley** from his studio on Warwick Road, Tyseley.

One evening in June 1960, as the Modernaires played on stage at the Wolverhampton **Scala**, word reached them that the manageress, **Brenda Bennett**, had received instant dismissal from her post. The Mods downed tools to plead Brenda's case. Ordered off the premises by the new regime, the Mods began to hastily pack what they could into **Brian Sharpe**'s Ford Farnham and **Mel Lees'** Consul. Arguments raged outside on the pavement as punters demanded refunds. "There was a bit of pushing and shouting and the next thing I know is I'm sailing through the air and straight through a plate glass window!" Mel winces as he recalls the night. "The Mods ended up tearing out of Wolverhampton and I ended up in hospital for the night! So much for loyalty!"

It wasn't long after that eventful evening when the Mods decided that a change of singer would be beneficial. Mel refused to be a part of **Dave Roberts'** removal from the line up and so severed his relationship with the Modernaires. That relationship had lasted three years and had seen them go from a start-up audition group to Casino champions. Ah well, such is the music business. Dave was replaced by a competent singer, **Micky Craven**, but it wasn't the same.

"We gave it a few months," recalls Brian Sharpe, "but then we started looking elsewhere."

The **Grasshoppers**, the Mods' main competitors, had no such problems. Indeed, they were out in front in the popularity stakes with their two cracking singers — **Micky Bakewell** and, **Brenda Bosworth** with her soulful style.

Micky Bakewell with the Modernaires at the Swan, Yardley

Brenda hadn't yet heard a new record by a young American artiste that was rapidly climbing the nation's charts in the summer of 1960. Brenda Lee's 'Sweet Nothin's' had entered the charts on the weekend that the Grasshoppers appeared at the **Centre Ballroom**, Coventry. "The crowd were convinced that I'd changed my name to Lee," says Brenda, "and were demanding for me do 'Sweet Nothin's' all night. It was only later in the week, when I heard the record that I realised not only the 'Brenda' tie up, but how uncannily alike our voices were. It was pure coincidence."

The **Modernaires** took deep breaths and approached **Micky Bakewell** with a view to getting him in as front man. "Wilf called me and asked me down to the **Sailors Return**, at the bottom of Garrison Lane." says Mick. "They were all set in the upstairs assembly room and I did Elvis's 'Mess Of Blues'. I had a pint up at the bar with the lads, they offered me the job — and I accepted."

The Vikings

In Nechells, the Wallace household was the talk of the area. With **Terry Wallace**'s group, the **Vikings**, getting out and about more, they became, as they say in showbiz circles, friends to the stars. It was a common occurrence on a Sunday evening to see the likes of Billy Fury, Carl Denver or Joe Brown coming out of the off-licence at Aston Cross and heading for Stuart Street and a good old knees up at the Wallace's. "Soon as they'd finish recording 'Thank Your Lucky Stars' at the Astoria building, our phone would go, and if we weren't working, it was party time!" sighed Terry.

The Vikings were working one Sunday evening, in early April of 1960, at a coffee bar in Coventry, just across from the famous Coventry Theatre.

"The big song of the day," recalls Terry, "was 'Twenty Flight Rock' by American star Eddie Cochran. It was my party-piece and I was doing it in this Coventry coffee bar when I became aware of a fellow in front of me, just staring at me. At the end of the song he applauded more loudly than anyone, and the party he was with began laughing. I suddenly recognised **Gene Vincent** and **Big Jim Sullivan**, the famous guitarist, in this fellow's party. The man in front of me? It was the man himself, **Eddie Cochran**. He waved to me and they all headed out of the coffee bar. They were on a national tour and had played Coventry that evening. I'd performed my hero's song to my hero and he'd applauded my efforts. A couple of days later he was gone — killed in a road crash in Chippenham."

Chapter Eight

QUIVERS DOWN THE BACKBONE

With their **Plaza** and **Ritz** ballrooms getting busier by the day, **Joe** and **Mary Regan** were more than happy with their world. "Everything seemed okay to me," said Joe "Charlie Simpson played and everybody danced – no problem."

"Then one night at the Ritz, a bloke said "Oy, Regan! It's about time you got a decent band down here." So I asked him to recommend one and he told me about this **Modernaires** band that were playing at the **Swan**, Yardley, every Monday and Thursday."

Joe went to the Swan and met with the Mods. "I booked them on the spot. I don't know if I liked the rock 'n' roll they were playing, but I was sure that it would go down well in my ballrooms."

He arranged for the Modernaires to appear at the Ritz every Saturday and Sunday evening, an arrangement that would soon see them at the Plaza, in Handsworth, the **Garryowen**, Small Heath, and the Regans' new venture, the **Old Hill Plaza**, on the Halesowen Road. Like the Handsworth Plaza, the new venue was a former picture house, but when the conversion was completed, it fulfilled a secret ambition that Joe had nursed since his younger days in London.

The Old Hill Plaza, just like the Cumberland Hotel, had a revolving stage. Now, when Joe Regan announced his attractions, they wouldn't make their entrances by climbing over amplifiers and drum kits. Now the bands would be all plugged in and ready to rock. Joe would shout "Okay boys, round you go!" crank a handle and indeed, round they would go. Unfortunately, most times the stage would come to a halt with such a jolt that cymbals, microphone stands and pints of beer balanced precariously on speaker cabinets would be sent flying!

Gerry Dorsey went down a storm at the Old Hill Plaza – even before he changed his name to Englebert Humperdink

A couple of miles South of Old Hill lies Halesowen, home of the **Juventors**, four lads led by **Mick Jones** of Windsor Road. They'd surfaced in '59 when guitarist Mick rounded up **Bill Dancock**, **Ralph Moore** and **Alan Newton** to embark on a grand tour that took in **Halesowen British Legion**, **Cradley Liberals Club** and, so as not to be biased, **Blackheath Labour club**.

Serious twisting to the Juventors at Summers Social Club, Halesowen

"Never had transport in them days," said Mick, "Didn't need it. I made a trolley with some pram wheels and we'd walk it." Alan Newton's brother, Clive, finally saved the day, and their legs, by offering to drive the Juventors around in his van. Now places like **Ludlow Town Hall** and **Pembridge Town Hall** were in reach and figuring in their diary.

Following their experiences at **Shard End British Legion** with drummer **Fred Allport** and his skulls, **Pete Green** and **Dezi Vyse** had appointed their own regular drummer. **Dave Mountney**, lived just off Camden Street and, like Pete and Dezi, was a regular at **Spring Hill Ice Rink**.

The Beachcombers

"Someone tipped us the wink that Dave was a decent drummer who played with the Air Training Corps." recalls Dezi. "He also, according to him, possessed his own kit. At our first rehearsal we saw the kit. It was a snare drum and an old cymbal, which could have doubled as a saucepan lid! But Dave also knew a bass player, **Pete McGinty**, so we had a band and we named it the **Beachcombers**. "We did every contest going," continued Dezi, "Anything to gain experience. We were in awe of the Modernaires and the Grasshoppers, but we believed in ourselves. We were also aware that we were probably the only band daring to perform some of our own material, as Peter Green was showing great promise as a song-writer. Finally the break came. It was at a talent show, maybe at the West End ballroom. Mrs Regan was there and engaged us as resident band at the **Handsworth Plaza**. We'd always looked up to the Modernaires with their big sound and their Ritz residency. Now, here we were, the Beachcombers, on the same level, over at the Plaza."

Beyond the Austin Motor Works and just off Bristol Road South, is Cliff Rock Road, where number 166 was the home of the **Wright** family. In 1959 the youngest of their two lads, **Nigel**, was given an accordion for Christmas. By the age of eleven, self taught, he mustered up enough nerve to play a few tunes for his pals at the **Essoldo**, Longbridge during the Saturday matinees. But in early '61, it was the guitar that grabbed his interest. One of his teachers at Colmores Farm School, Mr Welsh, organised a guitar club and Nigel enthusiastically enrolled.

"The first week," Nigel recalls, "There were about twenty of us lads. Next week ten, the week after, just me. The week after that I was giving Mr Welsh a lesson or two!" Nigel also taught his older brother **Rodney**, and they were soon joined by **Euan Rose** from Cofton Road Longbridge, with his drums. On bass, from Sir Hiltons Road in downtown West Heath, came **Roy Austin**. All they needed was a vocalist and **Graham Ashford** obliged, changing his name to **Buddy**

The back garden of the Wright family Eko's with music

Ash. And the band? They were called the **Eko's**. Ordering powder blue suits from **Colliers**, Northfield, just across from the Black Horse, the Ekos were soon picking up regular bookings at venues like **Cofton Community Centre**, **Cofton Hackett Village Hall** and the **Rubery Co-Op Rooms**. Summer evenings would see the Eko's rehearsing in the back garden of the Wright household. "We'd play all the Shadows stuff like 'Apache' with Euan thumping the tom-toms," recalls Nigel, "and at the end we'd get a more than polite round of applause from the neighbours, who'd be out dancing around in the back gardens!"

Over in Nechells, at the **Vikings** camp, the lads were experiencing immense sadness within the band. **John Kirby**, the guitarist who had replaced **Paul Evans**, had broken his neck in a horrific car smash and been permanently paralysed. After that most unfortunate accident however, John demonstrated tremendous spirit and inner strength. He put his creative efforts into horticulture, and developed a new fuschia, naming it **Cheryl** after **Terry Wallace**'s wife.

Worried about his professional career prospects, **Bobby Valentine**, the Vikings' vocalist, suddenly announced his retirement from pop music. He hung up his shiny suit, washed the Brylcream from his hair and returned to being plain Robert Hughes, the assistant registrar of births, deaths and marriages at the Broad Street offices. That allowed the spotlight to fall on **Keith Powell**, who transferred from the **Jaymen** to front the Vikings. Obviously with Keith came his father, 'Mr No-Nonsense' himself, **Jim Powell**, who would now take over management of the Vikings. With Jim Powell in the driving seat, the Vikings took on a whole new lease of life. As well as venturing up to the Potteries to Burslem and Hanley then over to Nantwich, they would travel to the East coast, to Great Yarmouth, where they would work for promoter **Jack Jay** (whose son Peter played drums in his own outfit, **Peter Jay and the JayWalkers**). As the Vikings popularity soared, so their date sheet became chock-a-block. So much so that Keith Powell decided he needed a holiday.

"Just a fortnight away from it all," said Keith, recalling the summer of '61.

The Vikings with Keith Powell at the Birmingham & Midland Institute

The band, however, were determined to fulfil their obligations. After all, there was money involved. **Barry Harbor**, their newly appointed

bass player, suggested that an old mate of his, from their days together at Saltley Grammar School, might be prepared to deputise for Keith. This friend was a wiry lad from Hodge Hill by the name of **Colin Tooley**. He was playing bass in a band called the **'G' Men**, but had been known to croon loves tune on the odd occasion. Colin Tooley embraced the chance of the limelight, even if it was only to be for a fortnight. It was agreed by all that when Keith returned home, Colin would be 'up the road, on his bike,' but it didn't quite work out that way.

"We were booked at the **Carlton**, Erdington," recalls **Terry Wallace**, "and in walks Colin Tooley. It was Keith's first night back and I said 'What's he doin' 'ere?' "

Colin Tooley was staying put. What is it they say about wild horses? He remained with the Vikings to sing *alongside* Keith Powell, and all with manager Jim Powell's approval. So, with the Vikings in their blue satin suits, and Keith in his purple suit, black shirt and white shoes, it seemed that a visit to **Chetwyn's** tailors was called for. There Colin was fitted out with a pink suit so all he needed now was a stage name.

"We thought something masculine would do it." laughed Terry, "To make up for the pink suit! John Wayne films were the *in* thing, so we initially thought of 'Duke Wayne', but eventually, to fall in with the Scandinavian theme of the Vikings, we went with 'Carl'." From then on it was Keith Powell, **Carl Wayne** and the Vikings. And it was rivalry! Friendly as it was, it was rivalry! After Keith had put over Hogey Carmichael's classic, 'Georgia', in those husky tones of his, so Carl would Charleston around and deliver 'Five Feet Two, Eyes of Blue!' If Carl won audience response, so Keith would grab the female attention with 'It's Now or Never,' and, as the screams died down, and the lighting paled, Carl Wayne would croon his party-piece, 'My Prayer is to Linger with You.' The upstairs room at the **Kings Head**, Bearwood, has never been the same since.

Vikings with Adam Faith backstage at Birmingham Town Hall

In the shadow of the Wimbush bakery, at 170 Green Lane, Small Heath, the **Yeates** family were in residence. The two lads of the household, **John**, the eldest, and **Brian**, had fallen heavily under the influence of rock 'n' roll music. Brian recalls that he, at the age of twelve, would stand outside Mrs Clare's parlour in Grange Road, listening intensely to **Wilf Clare's Gladiators** rehearsing their skiffle songs. By the late fifties, he'd even managed to pick **Johnny Carroll**'s brains and learn a few chords from that 'cheeky chappie,' as had big brother John. Much to the envy of Brian, brother John had joined a band, **Micky Harris and the Hawks**. Like any typical younger brother, Brian would follow John everywhere, turning up at practically every engagement the band performed at. "I'd just stand and watch everything they did, and if I wasn't at the gig, I'd be at home practising," said Brian.

Micky Harris & the Hawks

Perseverance paid off for Brian when, not quite seventeen years of age, he was invited into the Hawks to play along on his guitar. These were proud days indeed for Brian Yeates. He'd always been tiny in build but he felt a good six feet tall at the bus stop with his guitar under his arm. Every Sunday evening at the corner of Green Lane and the Coventry Road he waited for the 58 bus to whisk him to the Sheldon picture house, where he would alight and march up to the **Lyndon** pub – the Hawks regular weekend engagement.

The **Detours** meanwhile, on their travels around Northfield, somehow lost their way and got separated from **Jimmy Powell**. When they made it back to base, which in their case was **Smokey Joe's** transport café, facing the Traveller's Rest pub, there was no Jimmy. He'd been invited to help the **Rockin' Ber-**

The Rockin' Berries at Alvechurch Village Hall

ries handle all the 'beefy' songs, leaving **Paul Hewitt** to do the tamer Cliff Richard stuff. Jimmy, always an ambitious lad, knew a good move when he saw one, and grabbed the opportunity with both hands. The cheeky kid from Forrell Grove, West Heath, knew only too well that the Rockin' Berries would soon present him with the opportunity to quit his job as a lathe operator at Coley Brothers, Kings Norton. **Colin Smith**, of the Detours, quit the sinking ship. Overnight he became **Carl Barron**, and headed for the slopes of the Lickeys where he found the **Eko's** waiting for him to replace **Buddy Ash**.

Carl Barron with the Eko's

In the **Sicilio** coffee bar at Five Ways (which was squeezed in between the corner of Ladywood Road and the grand entrance of King Edward's School) sat **Mel Lees**, the former roadie-come-manager of the **Modernaires**. It was the summer of '61 and Mel, now working at Smart's, Wrentham Street, had taken a flat in Greenfield Road, Harborne. In his spare time he'd wander up through leafy Edgbaston to take coffee at the Sicilio. On this particular afternoon, as he sat, softly whistling through his repertoire, he was aware of two lads 'eyeing him up' and whispering to each other. Mel, always a shrewd man of the world, braced himself for action as the lads edged towards him. As it happened, he had nothing to fear. The two introduced themselves as **Jimmy Holden** and **Roy Bates** of the **Dominettes**. They'd recognised Mel from the time on Margate Pier when they had played a couple of numbers with the Mods and **Steve Gibbons**, only to finance the remainder of their stay by picking potatoes.

"They quickly came to the point," said Mel. "Was I interested in lending a hand to the Dominettes, as I had done with the Modernaires in their early days? I agreed and found myself helping them carry their bits of equipment from out of the Sicilio, round past the Children's Hospital and down to **Vincent Hall** in Ladywood, where they were appearing. The Dominettes were as rough as old boots. Like chalk and cheese to the Mods. Their gear was worth about three quid, but were they exciting! They knocked me out!"

Steve Gibbons with the Dominettes at the Scala, Wolverhampton

What Mel heard was a bunch of lads letting go with raunchy rhythm and blues. "**Steve Gibbons** did 'Muleskinner Blues' and there was sawdust in his vocal chords. He looked so mean and moody. Always the rebel was Steve. He was never in the *shiny suit brigade!*" Mel added with a wry smile.

Even so, the Dominettes did have to smarten up their act a little when gigs like the Scala started coming their way — stage jackets, tailor made in Wolverhampton by **Lester's**, and new amplifiers from **Grensall's**.

A little smarter, maybe, but their music was as dangerous as ever. When they played the **Lucas Social Club** in Hockley, the tickets bore the clear warning — 'Teen Dance. Jiving to the Dominettes. *No Straight Dancing.*'

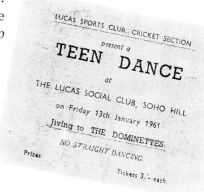

At about six-thirty on Sunday evenings in Brownhills, fans would start queuing to see the band roll up in their chauffeur driven car — a rare and magnificent Borgward Izabella, complete with running boards — to play the **Station** pub. "What a car that was!" Steve Gibbons recalls, "We towed a trailer with all the gear in, and on the back of it we'd painted *The Dynamic Dominettes*!"

Under the watchful eye of the licensee (and ex-boxer), Ron, the Brownhills crowd would go doo-lally to the band's versions of 'La Bamba', 'You've Got what it Takes' and the all time favourite 'Lipstick, Powder and Paint.'

"Germany calling!" announced a voice, accompanied by a knock on **Danny King**'s dressing room door. This wasn't Lord Haw-Haw however, but promoter **Reg Calvert**, backstage at **Banbury Winter Gardens**, one of Reg's regular rock 'n' roll venues. **Danny and the Royals**, **Tommy Owen**, **Garth Quirk** and **Barney Day**, soaked in perspiration following a heavy set, were sat enjoying a pint. Reg introduced the guest he had brought with him — **Peter Eckhorn**, a club owner from Hamburg. Peter had tried out a couple of British rock 'n' roll bands at his club, the **Top Ten**, and they had worked so well that he was on the look out for a few more. Peter Eckhorn made it clear that he wanted Danny King and the Royals to take the next stint at his club.

Danny King & the Royals at Snow Hill Station, bound for the Top Ten

"We didn't need asking a second time," said Tommy Owen, "First thing Monday, the notices went in at work and in no time we were off to the Reeperbahn!"

On arrival in Hamburg, Peter Eckhorn showed them the sights, let them relax for a day or so and then put Danny and the Royals to work at the Top Ten club, wishing them as much success as the previous band. A nice wish — to have as much success as the Beatles!

Life wasn't quite so exciting for **Bobby Hill and the Dominators**, but they were on the road and doin' it, which was all that matered. "Every Sunday night we'd do the **Tile Cross Youth Club**," **Greg Masters** recalls.

"My parents, by then, were back in the pub game at the Forge, corner of Fazeley Street. We'd make it back to the pub, after the gig for some supper. **Roger Hill** would always have Weetabix *and* Shredded Wheat all mixed together! My Mom used to heave," Greg continues, "So anyway, we had this idea to put our own dances on. Cut out the middle man, so to speak. We hired the church hall by Hazel's Funeral Directors, on Erdington High Street. The old ambulance broke down so we lugged the gear up on a pram. Nearly killed us! Any road, we started playing and people came in and we took a nice few bob on the door. It was turned ten o'clock and we thought we'd struck gold. Then the fight started! There were chairs and tables flying everywhere. We stopped and hid behind the curtains to keep out of the way. The people from the hall ended up having all the door money off us to pay for the busted furniture. That was the end of our enterprising days!"

Not content with the flamboyant stage clothes the **Rebels** were sporting, **El Riot (Ray Thomas)** had the idea of shaking just a little sparkling confetti into his black wavy hair, prior to taking the stage.

The Rockin' Berries

"It looked terrific. The birds used to go barmy," recalls **Bob Sheward**, the Rebels drummer. "There'd be us in these bandit outfits and Ray with these sparkly bits in his hair. We were on at the **Town Hall**. The compere was about to announce us and Ray was off-stage, holding the carton of confetti over his head and was about to sprinkle it on. **John Singer** put his head round the door and shouted,

"Hurry up lads!" Ray nearly jumped out of his skin. The top came off the carton and the whole lot, all this sparkly confetti, cascaded down into his hair. He just rubbed the lot in! El Riot walked on stage looking like a Christmas tree! All shiny glitter! The audience went crackers!"

The **Rockin' Berries** were now a real 'gritty' rhythm and blues outfit, with the 'grizzly bear' himself, **Jimmy Powell**, rasping out hard hitting songs like the Larry Williams number 'She Said Yeah.' Jimmy, for reasons known only to himself, began using the stage name of **Bobby Thomson**. It was a strange fluke that four years later, into their ranks would come a Liverpudlian — his name — Bobby Thomson!

Bobby tells the story as only a Scouser can. "When I first came down to join the Berries, **Terry Bond**'s family put me up at their house in Sir Hilton's Road, West Heath. I was struggling up the stairs with my suitcase and I saw a poster on the wall — *'The Rockin' Berries, featuring Bobby Thompson!'* I said to Terry, 'Ay! Bit premature der don't you think?' "

Anyway, back to 1961, and some news that was going to give the Berries their next shake-up. An offer of three months work in Germany had arrived and it meant decisions had to be made.

"I'd gone as far as I could," said **Paul Hewitt**, their 'pop' vocalist. "I was at the Austin. I had a good job and I was about to get married. It had to be bye-bye Berries"

Turning professional — Jimmy Powell

So band-leader **Dougie Thompson** turned his attention once more to **Clive Lea**, the lad he'd spotted a couple of years earlier at Rubery Social club. Then, Dougie had got nothing to offer the shy lad with the flare for impersonations, but it was a different story now. There was a contract — there was the glamour of showbiz — there was a whole world outside of Longbridge waiting to be discovered. Clive agreed to join, and in November '61, he set off with the Rockin' Berries in search of fame and fortune in Germany.

Jimmy Powell reckoned his career move might be worth a bit of publicity, so before he left Coley Brothers in Kings Norton, he gave the story to the Birmingham Mail. The article read, *'Jimmy Powell quits his job as a seven pounds a week lathe operator to sing with the Rockin' Berries in Germany at thirty pounds a week!'*

Fellow 'Berry' **Dennis Ryland** chuckled to himself. "That's my Jimmy," he laughed. "Always had to stick a tenner on the top!"

Chapter Nine

OH! YOU'RE LOOKIN' GOOD!

The Autumn of '61 had seen a recording, 'The Twist', which promoted a new dance of the same name, show briefly on the hit parade, the artiste being one Chubby Checker. Columbia Records were not perturbed by low sales and rush released a follow-up in time for the important seasonal market. That record, 'Let's Twist Again', found itself within reach of the nation's top five records as Britain *Gay Gordoned* into '62.

In Birmingham's ballrooms and pub function rooms, dance-floors came alive with folks going 'round and round and up and down,' and in homes across the city, even some fathers would demonstrate their abilities with a quick little twist in the corner on the linoleum, to show how in-touch they were with what was going on in the wonderful world of the young.

The dance had apparently originated in certain 'gentlemen only' clubs that made up New York's night life, and the lyric of the Sam Cooke classic, 'Twistin' the Night Away', reflected the spirit of the 'Big Apple' as it told of people who were so gay, they were twisting the night away.

Perhaps ignorance was bliss to thoroughbred Brummies who cared little for New York jive talk as the crowds at the **Handsworth Plaza** roared their approval of the **Beachcombers**, the new resident band that Mr and Mrs Regan had brought in to cater for the twisters.

Always the shrewd business lady, Mrs Regan announced that a grand talent contest was to be held at the Handsworth Plaza and contestants would be provided with superb musical accompaniment from the **Charlie Simpson Orchestra**.

"The early heats were a great success," **Dezi Vyse** of the Beachcombers recalls, "The crowds piled in and loved every second. Then came the Grand Final. There were three acts competing. The first act was two girls who did a 'Sisters' routine, like the Beverley Sisters. Next was a middle aged bloke who played the clarinet and last was a

Bobby Darin sound-alike male vocalist. Joe Regan was on stage to compere the contest and announced to a packed Plaza audience that part of the first prize was the chance to join the Beachcombers! The crowd, the contestants all went berserk! What a prize! The only thing was that we in the Beachcombers knew nothing of such an arrangement!"

The band scooted upstairs into what had been the projection room of the old Rookery cinema to get a bird's eye view of the contest.

"We were hanging out of the hatch in the wall, sweating buckets," chuckled Dezi, "What if the girls won? Worse still, what if the 'Acker Bilk' bloke won? When the male vocalist came on we dropped to our knees and prayed for him!"

Fortunately for them, the vocalist, **John Ship**, from Willes Road, Winson Green, put in an excellent performance and found himself, overnight, as the new featured vocalist with the Beachcombers. Next day, John Ship became singing sensation — **Bobby Coral** — and was ushered by Pete Green's uncle-come-band-manager, **Phil Peters**, to a high class tailor to be measured for a silky blue stage suit that cost nearly a hundred pounds, an absolute fortune in those days.

"So it's Bobby's debut with us at the Plaza," says Dezi, shaking his head. "Bobby was chain smoking in the dressing room when Pete announced him on stage. Bobby put out his cigarette with his fingertips

Bobby Carol & Johnny Neal with the Modernaires at Handsworth Plaza

Roger Bruce — source of records & knowledge to many a Birmingham band

and dropped the remnants into his jacket pocket. Halfway through the first number and we smelled smoke. Bobby was on fire! We had to stop playing and smother him!"

The **Ritz**, over in Kings Heath, was now all about the **Modernaires**. **Roger Bruce**, who supplied the Modernaires with all the latest releases from his Bordesley Green record shop, remembers those days so well.

"The Modernaires were my life. I *swear* it!" he emphasizes. "I followed them everywhere. Monday it was the **Swan**, Yardley. Tuesday, the **Harlequin**, Shard End, Wednesday, the **Old Hill Plaza**. Thursday, back to the Swan. Friday, it was the **Garryowen** in Wordsworth Road, and Saturday and Sunday, the **Ritz**! Then Monday we'd start all over again!"

It seems the Modernaires were as popular as the Twist itself. They now had acquired a piece of equipment that set them so far ahead of any other local band.

"They had an *echo chamber*!" exclaims **Steve Gibbons**, still in a state of shock after all the years that have passed. "*Nobody* had an echo in those days and it made them sound like nothing on earth! It was incredible! The sax player, Moss, used to do 'Rockin' Goose', and he'd do the 'goose' sound by taking the mouthpiece off his sax and just blowing down that into the mic! And with the echo on full! It used to bounce round the Ritz like nobody's business!"

Bouncing around Sparkhill in '61 were two lads who were about to leave Moseley Grammar School and take their place in Brum society. **Beverley Bevan**, of 803, Stratford Road, Sparkhill, simply 'Bev' to his mates, had inherited his late father's talent as a drummer, whilst the studious one of the two, **Phil Ackrill**, from Fulham Road, across from the Mermaid, had taken up the guitar. Being the fashion conscious pair that they were, Bev and Phil had managed to win the friendship of the young man who worked at Zissman's, the gents' outfitters, on the corner of Stoney Lane, **Ronnie Smith**.

"Ronnie, like Bev, was a go getter — driving force," says Phil Ackrill, "He put a band together with Bev, me and **Tony Withers**, who actually had an *electric* guitar. It was the **Renegades** first and then we changed it to **Ronnie and the Senators**. We used to practise at Bev's mom's shop, where they lived on Stratford Road. **Alan Thompson** had a builders yard over from Ladypool Road. He also had an A35 van, and he'd transport us around to places like

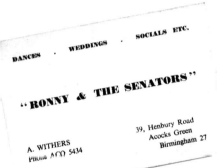

DANCES · WEDDINGS · SOCIALS ETC.

"RONNY & THE SENATORS"

39, Henbury Road
Acocks Green
Birmingham 27

A. WITHERS
Phone ACO 5434

Shirley Annexe, Hall Green Church Youth Club. Fifty bob between us! And then — wait for it — the **Las Vegas Coffee Bar**, down Summer Row, which for us, was a big deal then."

Sunday afternoons would see Bev and Phil at Ronnie Smith's parents house, in Prince Of Wales Lane, Warstock, where the three of them would play the Presley and Gene Vincent records full blast on Ronnie's Dansette player as Mr Smith senior struggled against the noise to take his Sunday afternoon snooze.

"He had such understanding parents," chuckled Phil.

On a pleasant Sunday lunchtime, at the bar in the smoke room of the **Beeches** pub, Hoggs Lane, Northfield, George Bache of Rubery, bought pop and crisps for his fourteen year old son and his three pals. However, he didn't take the refreshments out into the beer garden, but instead passed the loaded tray over to the musicians, **Johnny Shane and the Rockin' Solitaires**. "We were only thirteen, maybe fourteen years of age and that was our first booking," says drummer **George Mills** proudly. "It was me, my cousin **Robert Mills** and **Dave Bache** on guitars. **Kenny Lowe** played bass and **Johnny Shane** was our sultry looking singer. By day he was **Maurice Press** and went to Colmores Farm School. We were all still at school. The whip-round got us four and a half quid that Sunday morning. The gaffer of the **George**, on Bristol Road, saw us. He must have liked what he saw because we played his pub every Monday night for ages."

The **Rockin' Berries** had arrived back in town from their German stint. They were now fully professional musicians and had a return engagement in Germany to look forward to. Their leader, **Dougie Thompson**, had heard that **Jack Goode**, the legendary producer of television pop shows, was in Birmingham, and talent scouting on behalf of **Decca Records**. Never one to hang around, Dougie made contact and the Rockin' Berries auditioned for Mr Goode, at the **ATV Studios** in Aston.

That afternoon the Berries

Johnny Shane & the Solitaires at Handsworth Plaza

ran through some raunchy, rhythm and blues songs for the cold and calculated man from the 'Smoke'. To an outsider, the music business is a very glamorous and rewarding profession to be in. The reality is that it breaks hearts and spirit time after time as rejection nearly always seems to rear its ugly head. As Dougie Thompson signalled for the lads to belt into another song, so Jack Goode rose from his seat and gestured that he'd heard enough.

"What do you think?" asked Dougie, wiping the perspiration from his forehead.

"Thanks for coming along, but you have to understand that there's a million groups out there," answered the Mighty Man, in the heartless way that only show-biz moguls can and do.

"Mind you," he continued, "I might be able to do something for the singer," nodding at **Jimmy Powell**.

Dougie Thompson's back was up. Dougie was the man who had dared to face those infamous teddy boys, the Brookes brothers, so many times during vicious fisticuffs at the Palace, Redditch. No one, not even Jack Goode, could dismiss Dougie so coldly.

"You're dealin' with the Rockin' Berries," he stated in true Musketeer fashion. "You take the band or nothing at all!"

"Now let's not be too 'asty," interrupted Jimmy Powell, as he waltzed the legendary producer to a quiet corner, "Me and Mr Goode have got a little business to attend to."

Waltzes and quicksteps were on **Ken Gallon**'s mind in early '62. Ken had taken on the responsibility of entertainment secretary at the **Ravenscroft Social Club**, in Grange Road, Small Heath.

Johnny King & the Diamonds

"We needed a band for a presentation night. A band that could mix it up a bit. You know, a few waltzes, foxtrots and a bit of rock-a-boogie," explained Ken.

"Only thing was, being a small club, we didn't have any money to pay them. At the time my wife, Iris, and I were living in Donnington House on the Meadway. Doreen, the girl who had the flat on the other side of the landing, had told Iris about her younger brother, Roy, starting up this band, the **Falcons**. Me and Iris went down to a hall in Lea Village, where they practised, to see if they were any good. They hadn't got a clue what a waltz was, so me and the missus started to waltz, counting 'one, two, three,' in time as we danced. Dennis, the drummer picked up the beat and then **Billy Martin**, the singer, began crooning 'Around the world I searched for you.' The guitarist, Roy, fumbled for a while but eventually got the chords going. Next, we did the quickstep. Same thing, Dennis gets the beat first, then Billy starts singing 'Hello Mary Lou, Goodbye heart,' with Roy joining in, 'til in the end it was like 'Come Dancing.' We booked the Falcons for nothing. They played great. Billy Martin knew how to put a ballad over. He was fabulous. Dennis kept the beat going and then Roy did a song he'd written, called 'Sandy'. The lads played us a bit of rock-a-boogie to wind up. We sent the tray round and we got eighteen quid for them! Yeah, that's right. It was **Roy Wood** with the Falcons. It was their first booking."

Mark Stuart & the Crestas at the Bournbrook, Selly Oak

Micky Harris and the Hawks were still hovering around at the Lyndon on Sunday evenings. "The only problem was," recalls **Brian Yeates**, "That Micky took his girlfriend to the Sheldon pictures every Sunday afternoon and he'd miss our first spot. I'd do the singing until he decided to arrive."

Eventually, the Hawks told Micky Harris not to rush his Ki-Ora because Brian was putting down his guitar and taking the vocalist job permanently.

"Nobody said anything to *me*! said Brian. "I just did what my brother John and the rest of the band told me to do!"

Brother John actually left at around this time to become **Johnny King** with his own band, the **Diamonds**. And little Brian? He bought himself some fancy stage wear from **Nelson House**, on Coventry Road and became **Mark Stuart**. The Hawks? They became the **Crestas**.

"As Mark Stuart and The Crestas, we really got going for it!" Brian remembers. "We used to open up with Duane Eddy's 'Earthquake'. We'd have our backs to the audience to start, then we'd hit it. **Archie Edwards** would be twanging his guitar, then, as we turned to face the audience, so **Johnny Beresford** would be playing a honkin' sax. We really let 'em have it! I'd been quite a gymnast at school, so I used to do the splits, handstands and cartwheels all over the place!"

Mark and the Crestas used the **Bournbrook** pub for rehearsals. As did **Mike Sheridan and the Nightriders**.

Says Brian "We'd be upstairs and Mike and the lads would use the downstairs lounge. Halfway through, I'd meet Mike and we'd swap lyrics and arrangements of whatever songs we were working on. It never occurred to us that the outcome would be that both bands would wind up with exactly the same repertoire! It was a plain simple 'help a mate' situation."

Following one rehearsal at the Bournbrook, the Crestas remained at the pub to play for the evening's rock 'n' roll session.

"I'd noticed a few 'townie' looking blokes up at the bar," said Brian, "and as we finished, one came over and asked if we knew where Navigation Street was. When I told him that we did, he said 'Good. I need you at my club tonight. It's called the **Bermuda**. You're on in an hour.' He didn't ask if we were available. He just took it for granted we'd do it, which we did. From then on we'd do anything for that bloke — **Eddie Fewtrell** — he was good to us and helped a lot of bands in those early days."

Pete Worrall alias **Danny Burns**, also has happy memories of the Bermuda Club. "We used to back the strippers!" he recalls. "We were only kids and we used to blush like crazy."

The strippers didn't make **Steve Gibbons and the Dominettes** blush. Their experiences took place at the **Grotto Club** at the bottom of Bromsgrove Street, next to the Black Swan pub.

"What a place that was!" enthuses Steve. "Down some steps. Knock three times and ask for Joe! It was all market blokes, I s'pose. We'd back the strippers and then meet them for a drink in the Black Swan after the show. The Grotto was run by the **Finn brothers**, **Martin**, who was a dentist in Gooch Street, **Gary** and **Micky**. Yeah, *Micky Finn!*"

The Dominettes, by this time, had moved their base from the **Sicilio** coffee bar on Five Ways to the **Firebird** in Carrs Lane.

"The Firebird was a jazz club basically," explains Steve Gibbons. "It was run by the trumpet player with the **Artesian Hall Stompers**, **Dan Pawson**, and his wife, **Maude**. "The punters were mainly beatniks. You know, polo necks and pipes. So we went down and asked Dan and Maude for a try out. They gave us a Tuesday and it was okay. The next Tuesday was wonderful and it went on from there. Every Tuesday, the Dominettes! we used to leave our gear there. It was our base. Every night we'd make it back to the Firebird for the last tot!"

Also into the odd tot or two was **Johnny Neal** and his new back up band, the **Starliners**, or, as they became known at Hamburg's **Star Club**, the *Bar*liners!

"**Reg Calvert** sent us out there," recalls Johnny, "and when we arrived, the **Beatles** were supporting **Gene Vincent** at the club — and we were all in awe of *Gene Vincent*! On our first night in Hamburg, we met the Beatles and did they make us welcome. They got us involved in their round. Phew! It was wild!" continues Johnny. "One of Gene Vincent's big stage numbers was 'Alley Oop'. Every time Gene sang the punchline, 'Alley Oop!,' **John Lennon** had us stand, raise our glasses and down a good slug of whiskey in one! We couldn't see straight for days!"

Gerry Levene and the Avengers were also seeing stars, but this was due more to pressure of work. **Ken Smith**, who had given the band their name at his promotion, the **Say Mama** at Sutton Coldfield, had become their full time agent. During the day he worked for Bell and Nicholson in the city centre, but the firm transferred Ken to their Merseyside offices. Always the hustler, Ken Smith soon began finding engagements around Cheshire and Merseyside for the Avengers and also **Mark Stuart and the Crestas**.

"Here's a sample of our worksheet," says Gerry, opening the Avengers 1962 diary. "Saturday, 30th March — morning show, **Gaumont**, Worcester; lunchtime, the **West End**, Suffolk Street, and on to the **Old Hill Plaza**, then to the **Wheatsheaf**, Sheldon for a private function — and then the **Moat House**, back of the Bull Ring! Five shows in one day! Next day, Sunday 31st — the **Star Ballroom**, Burton and then **Tamworth Assembly Rooms**! Following night, **Hall Green Tech**! Next night **Queen's Head**, Erdington. It just went on and on and on! We all loved it, but I was wondering just how long could we carry on at that pace.

It was a pace that **Phil Ackrill** and **Bev Bevan** would have envied. Phil had a job as a bank clerk with Barclays whereas Bev, along with a school chum, **Bob Davis**, who everyone, except his mother, referred to as Jasper, had started work at the Beehive department store in Birmingham.

"I remember Jasper walking round looking totally bewildered," says Phil. "The boss at the Beehive had told him to report for duty on the Manchester counter and he was worried how he was going to get home 'cause the Midland Reds didn't go that far. Bev hadn't the heart to explain that the Manchester counter was, in fact, the linen department!

Providing a crust for Bev & Jasper — the Beehive

Bev Bevan still had a bit of a hankering for the straight life. The Bee-hive were running a management course and Bev enrolled with a fair amount of enthusiasm. The course was held at **Rackhams** department store every Tuesday evening, outside of working hours, and it was here that Bev Bevan met up with a young Rackhams employee, **Brian Hines**.

"Brian had this wonderful job in the record department at Rackhams," explained Phil Ackrill. "He made up compilation tapes all day! You know, 'Muzak' to be played in the store! What a job! But he wanted out."

Brian Hines had told Bev all about his band Johnny Dean and the Dominators, but good as they were, the band had no ambition to progress out of Birmingham and into the big world that was just waiting for Brian Hines, or as he was to become, **Denny Laine**, to arrive.

Johnny Dean & the Diplomats at the Nelson, Warwick

"Me and Bev went to see the **Dominators** at an Irish social club in Digbeth," recalls Phil. "Afterwards Brian walked home with us. Yeah, walked! All the way up Stratford Road. As we walked we plotted our future. By the time we reached the Mermaid, where Brian branched off for Tyseley, we had our new band named. It was to be **Denny Laine and the Diplomats** — Brian, or from then on Denny, on lead, me on rhythm, Bev on drums and from the Dominators, on

bass, **Dave Wheeland**, who Bev had christened 'Wongy'. Why Wongy? Well he had Chinese eyes, didn't he!"

The Diplomats set to work immediately. First port of call was **Stan the Van**, on Ladypool Road, where they purchased a Bedford Dormobile for thirty pounds, and next, a visit to the caretaker at the school hall next to Sparkhill Baths, to arrange for rehearsals.

"Looking back, I s'pose it was only simple but at the time it felt and sounded great. Denny was very much into music. It was all good stuff."

One of their first engagements as Denny Laine and the Diplomats was at **Maney Hall**, Sutton Coldfield. A venue that Denny had played quite a few times with the Dominators. Consequently, he was well known to the **Say Mama** crowd and the band did the proverbial 'stormer.'

Denny Lane & the Diplomats at the Springfield Ballroom, Sparkhill

"The audience were going barmy." said Phil. "They were demanding something and weren't going to leave until they'd had it. Denny turned to me and said. 'It's no good, I'll have to do it. Hold my guitar.' Then he leapt off the stage and broke into backflips and somersaults. The crowd were going berserk. Of course they'd seen it before, but *we* hadn't! Denny was cart-wheeling round the room. Legs whizzin' round like helicopter blades. He was back-flipping all over the place. When he made it back to the stage, I asked him if he expected the band to join in the routine!"

At last the time had come for the **Rockin' Berries** to set off again for Germany. No one was more happy than **Chuck Botfield**. "I'd taken a job as a driver and deliveryman at Munn's, in Camden Street. They did photographic film processing. I told the boss I wasn't happy with the way things had developed. He didn't get the gag and I knew then it was all over. I made my excuses and left."

On completion of their initial contract, an offer for the band to remain in Germany was made, but **Dougie Thompson** was feeling that with a wife and kids to keep, his place was back in West Heath and **Dennis Ryland** was missing the basic luxuries in life such as bread and shoes.

"Early in the week, we'd eat steak dinners. They were twelve bob a time and up 'ere," said Dennis, gesturing the height of the plateful of food piled to just under his chin. "As the days passed, you started running short of the readies, so you'd make do with pancakes."

Jimmy Powell too, was keen to get back and make a go of things in his hometown, Birmingham.

So it was 'auf Wiedersehen' to Germany for the three dissenters, leaving Chuck, **Clive Lea**, **Terry Bond** and **Tim Munns** to soldier on in Hamburg.

On arrival home, Dennis found employment at the Austin, Longbridge. "I asked them for a job on transport so I'd be able to brag a lift home!" he laughed.

Dougie Thompson set up a promotions and entertainment agency that traded from an office in Dale End, specialising, funnily enough, in sending young musicians to Germany in search of the great rock 'n' roll dream. Jimmy Powell, assisted by **Jack Goode**, rejoiced in the accolade of being the first 'Brumbeat' recording artiste to enjoy a commercial release — his version of 'Sugar Babe' on the **Decca** label.

Chapter Ten

HEY JACK, HIT THE ROAD!

Steve Horton still chuckles at the memory of his first meeting with **Denny Laine**, "I'd never seen a bloke with orange hair before!" Steve had been playing bass with a Sheldon outfit, **Clive and the Dominators** (not to be confused with Johnny Dean's lot) but with ambition in his heart and a few quid in his pocket, he headed for the bright lights of London to be a professional backing musician for the singer **Jackie Lynton**. He shared a room with fellow Brummie, Mike Pinder, who was the pianist with the band at the time.

"Whether it was being away from Brum at such a young age or the feeling that I just wasn't good enough, I don't know, but I came home and got a job at **Zissman's** in Dale End," says Steve, "Anyway, into the shop came this bloke with his hair dyed orange. He was after a shirt. We got talking. He was in a band, the **Diplomats**, and they all had their hair dyed the same colour! I told him I played bass and he mentioned that their bass man, was emigrating to Australia. Did I fancy a go?"

Denny Laine & the Diplomats

Steve Horton *did* fancy a go, and became the replacement in the Diplomats for **Wongy Wheeland**. Fortunately for Steve, the lads decided that orange hair was out of fashion and blonde was the hue of the future. With the assistance of Hall Green hairdresser **Joe McGann**, the colour transformations took place. Not content with that gimmick, the band members passed themselves off to their public as two sets of cousins. Steve became

Sonny Laine to pass himself off as Denny's cousin. **Phil Ackrill** and **Bev Bevan** both took the surname of **Ralston** and, showing complete commitment, gave up their day jobs.

Cousins or not, natural blondes or not, the Diplomats, now fully pro, were 'the business', appearing regularly at the **Solihull Civic Hall** every Monday and the **Tyburn House**, Erdington, every Tuesday.

Phil Ackrill recalls, "We'd pop our twelve quid booking fee into the Strepsils tin that was on the dashboard as we pulled off the car park. That paid the expenses for the week!"

The Diplomats would also be a regular feature at the **Star Ballroom**, over the top of Burton's on Stratford Road, and the girls at the **Adelphi**, New Street, West Bromwich just went overboard for the four blonde wandering minstrels.

"The Adelphi times were great," Steve Horton recalls with fondness. "We'd always stop on the way home to play ten pin bowling at the alley by the Baggies ground. No rush. They were open all night."

Whenever they appeared at the **Springfield**, Sparkhill, Steve remembers, the Diplomats always seemed to acquire a roadie.

"It was Bev and Phil's mate, Jasper. He'd grab a mic stand or a guitar from the back of the van and glide past the doorman without paying. Once he was in, he was in! No coming back for more equipment as I recall. Jasper was working for Colgate, but he wanted to set up on his own, doing the markets, selling shampoo. He had this idea of making gallons of the stuff in his bath and bottling it up to sell down the Bull Ring."

One of the Bull Ring's most famous traders was the 'Banana King' himself, the man who could always be seen weaving in and out of the stalls wearing a carnation in his jacket lapel — Mr **Rob Pryke**.

In 1961, Mr Pryke, had acquired for himself a license to print money. In other words he'd become the proprietor of a betting office, an occupation that had only recently become legal. Early in 1962, not content with just flogging bananas or skinning punters, he ventured into the glamorous world of night clubs by launching his own establishment, the **Moat House**, in Moat Row, at the back of the Bull Ring.

The Moat House quickly became the 'in' place for the creme de la creme of Birmingham's night-owlers. Sports personalities and stars of stage and screen would freely rub shoulders with the apres-theatre clientele and market workers who, in the wee small hours of the morning, would stagger down the stairs of the Moat House club and find their barrows waiting for them!

Brian Betteridge of **El Riot and the Rebels** has happy memories of the Moat House. "We were just plugging in to start playing when Mrs Pryke came to the stage. Winking at me she said, 'Play your best numbers first, there's someone from the telly up the bar.' It turned out to be the **Lunchbox** producer **John Pullen**, and he booked us for a few spots on the show. It was a

Eddie Calvert with Lunchbox regulars El Riot & the Rebels

great break. The Rebels would do an instrumental to close the first half, then after the adverts **Ray Thomas**, in all his El Riot glory, would do a song. Being regulars on the television did wonders for the bookings!"

Indeed as a result of their appearing on Lunchbox, El Riot and his Rebels found themselves in demand at the **Tower Ballroom**, sharing the bandstand with Lunchbox fave raves, **Jerry Allen and his Trio**. More often than not, during Jerry's final set the Riot gang would live up to their name, coming back on stage to jam with the band in a musical rampage.

Not quite as salubrious as the Tower, but just as exciting, was the Golden Eagle pub, a daunting looking building in Hill Street, on the corner of Swallow Street. During the Second World War, the pub had been one of the recognised city centre hangouts for American servicemen. With the GIs long gone, all that remained were memories of nylons, bubble gum, vicious fights and American music; especially that real bluesy type of stuff performed by black Americans and favoured by the early sixties student fraternity.

Spencer Davis was such a student. A Swansea lad, he'd arrived in Birmingham in 1960 to study German at Birmingham University. A real fan of the skiffle approach to the blues, he had become a regular customer at the Golden Eagle on Wednesday evenings when the **Rhythm Unlimited Club** would be meeting in the upstairs function room. On the odd occasion, the **Excelsior Jazz Band** would play the gig and Spencer would fill the interval spot, performing solo as a vocalist and guitarist with his repertoire of 'railroad' songs. It was here that the young Welsh student met up with the drummer of the Excelsiors. A chap from Nottingham called **Pete York**, who was living in Harborne whilst completing an apprenticeship at Guest, Keen and Nettlefold in Winson Green.

Although they didn't know it at the time, Spencer Davis and Pete York would be forming a blues combo with two brothers from Atlantic Road, Kingstanding. The elder brother, **Mervyn 'Muff' Winwood** was born in '43 and five years later his mother, Lillian, presented him with a baby brother, **Stephen**. From day one, the brothers were surrounded by the sound of music as their father, Lawrence, was a semi-professional saxophone player with various dance bands around the city. He also possessed a jazz and blues record collection that was second to none. If Mr Winwood wasn't practising his pieces, the records would be playing. Consequently Steve and Muff needed little encouragement to take up music as a serious subject.

Ticket away Muff

By 1960, Muff was already in operation with his own band, the **Muff Woody Jazz Band**, playing at the school hops of Great Barr Comprehensive and even surviving a performance at the **Birmingham Arms** in Sherlock Street, with limbs still intact. Steve, now highly proficient on piano, was the star pupil of **Tom Knowles**, a teacher who ran a guitar class during the lunchtimes at school. It was obvious that a career in music awaited the Winwoods, but with Steve still only twelve years of age, the upstairs room of the Golden Eagle pub would have to wait awhile for their appearance.

It is said that you could set your clock by the **Yeates**' brothers. **John** and **Brian** of Green Lane, Small Heath would arrive home at exactly the same time for their evening meal and then jostle for positions around the washbasin. No sooner had the last strands of hair had been Brylcreamed into place than two Commer vans would roll up outside. One vehicle would have aboard the **Diamonds** whilst the other carried the **Crestas**.

"The horns used to 'pip' more or less in sync, and out of the front door of number 170 would skip Brian, alias **Mark Stuart**, followed by John, alias **Johnny King**," chuckled **Tim Bellamy**, the Diamonds' drummer. "It got as they could tell which 'pip' was the Diamonds' 'pip' and which 'pip' was the Crestas'."

Max 'the Nub' Griffiths, the lead guitarist with the **Nightriders**, said 'toodle pip' to Mike Sheridan around this time and set about starting up a new band — the **Rockin' D'fenders**.

"Thinking about it, it wasn't the most amicable of partings," Mike remembers. "The Nightriders had been Max's band back in the **Billy King** days, but Max got his own thing going eventually."

Into the Nightriders came **Alan Johnson**, or, to friends, associates and his customers at Burton's, the tailors in Corporation Street, where he was the manager — **Big Al**.

"Big Al was a great rock 'n' roll player," said Mike. "Very much into Gene Vincent. At that time we did a lot of work supporting Gene Vincent and of course Big Al knew all the lead breaks note for note. Gene thought the world of Big Al. Whenever Gene Vincent played round here he always stayed at Big Al's house up on the Ridgeway, by Stockland Green."

The friendly rivalry that existed between **Carl Wayne** and **Keith Powell** was becoming a little hostile. "It was just petty jealousies." said Keith. "We were two young blokes, typical Brummies, who were both singing in one of Birmingham's most popular outfits. We'd argue over who sang what and when. Who'd open. Who'd close. Who'd take which girl home. All total irrelevant stuff, but we were just boys in a very exciting world. Myself and Carl today are the greatest of mates, but then, back in '62, it was heavy!"

Carl Wayne & the Vikings

Terry Wallace recalls, "It had been coming to the boil for a few weeks. We were outside my house in Nechells. It was about two o'clock in the morning and the balloon went up. They started shouting at each other. The neighbours called the coppers even though it was only shouting. That was it. Keith left and took his old man with him."

From then on it was simply **Carl Wayne and the Vikings**. The end of the rainbow was in sight, and with the pot of gold figuring heavily in their dreams, the Vikings decided to introduce a little light comedy into their stage performances.

"Carl reckoned he could 'do' Hilda

Baker," Terry Wallace chuckled. "So he'd make his entrance in full drag regalia, with balloons up the front of his cardigan. He'd pat the back of his hairnet and mutter, in a passable Lancashire accent, those immortal words, 'Be soon, I say, be soon! Aye! She knows, you know!'"

What a knockout! Routines like that should be shared with the world. This was hard hitting stuff that should not, in any way, be confined to the rehearsal room. Those were the Vikings' feelings as they made their way to the **Essoldo** cinema, at Quinton. Bursting with confidence they took to the stage to face their audience. An audience that was, as they found out later, the 1962 version of the Quinton Mob.

"We'd have been alright if we'd have just worked in the glow of the usherettes' torches, but when the spotlights went on full we were sitting ducks," mused Terry Wallace. "As soon we struck into the first song, we came under heavy fire of orange peel, apple cores and toffees." Terry dabbed the tip of his finger on his tongue and drew a line on the table to help illustrate their battle tactics. "We felt that if we could hold the lower circle and its flanks until 'My Prayer,' we'd be okay as we were out of the balcony's range. However, halfway through 'Five Feet Two, Eyes of Blue' we lost **Graham Hollis**, our drummer. Both ice cream queues had sneaked past our front line and he was getting it from both sides. Carl thought that the Hilda Baker routine would pull it round but it just made things worse. When they started using pop cartons and half eaten ice-lollies we took the only option we had. We legged it straight out the place!"

Discomfort of another kind was awaiting **Danny King and the Royals** in London. "We'd got two nights down the Smoke," **Tommy Owen** explained. "The first was at the **Top Twenty Club** in Peckham and the following night we were in Camberley. We drove down in two A35 cars. We were in the first car with guitars and suitcases piled on our laps. The drums and the amps were in the second car. After the first show, at the Top Twenty, we realised we hadn't anywhere to stay, so we drove into Leicester Square and parked at the road side. We tried to sleep with all the guitars, overnight bags, everything piled on us, as we sat bolt upright in this little A35! Next morning, our legs couldn't support us! Absolute agony! Rock 'n' roll — a glamorous profession? Do me a favour!"

Rock 'n' roll was starting to become a little more glamorous for the four Liverpool lads that Danny King and the Royals had followed into Hamburg's **Top Ten Club** a year earlier. Having been humiliated by **Decca** the **Beatles** had signed to **Parlophone Records**, a minor label within the **EMI** organisation. The major label within that organisation was **Columbia Records**, whose head of the Artists and

Repertoire department was **Norrie Paramour**. His catalogue of artistes included the bowler hatted Acker Bilk and his Paramount Jazz Band, Frank Ifield (the yodelling milkman), the teenaged Helen Shapiro, and the 'hottest' act of all, Cliff Richard. Along with his Shadows, he reflected the true image of the typical British teenager. They didn't drink, smoke or swear and they were always doing free shows in youth clubs in aid of worthy causes. At least that's how it was according to their film scripts.

With the release of their first single imminent, the Beatles were embarking on engagements around the provinces. Sutton Coldfield's very own version of the Liverpool Cavern club, the **Say Mama** was one such calling point for them.

Danny Burns

Gerry Levene tells it how it was. "**Ken Smith** was paying the Beatles fifty quid. I'd worked with them up in Liverpool and seen them in action. The audiences would place presents and cards at their feet. At **Maney Hall** with the Avengers, we opened, gave it our best shot and got out the way. The Beatles came on and whoosh!"

Tommy Burton Combo

Danny Burns and his Phantoms arrived to catch the end of the Beatles set. "We were playing in town first and were booked to play when they had finished." Danny Burns, recalls. "We got there and saw them tearing the place apart. As we went on they were off to Tamworth. I think half of Sutton went after them. We were a bit of an anti-climax after that!"

Wednesfield lad **Mac Bailey**, the guitarist with Wolverhampton's **Tommy Burton Combo**, picks up the trail, "Tommy Burton was the hero of the Black Country with his boogie-woogie piano playing and his natural comedy. We pulled up outside the **Adelphi Ballroom** in West Bromwich and the poster said, 'Tonight! The Beatles! Tommy Burton Combo! The **Grasshoppers**!' Tommy looked at me and said, 'Blimey, we're on with a load of insects!' "

Brenda Bosworth, of the Grasshoppers remembers that night very well. "Tommy Burton and us always went down a storm at the Adelphi. We'd never heard of the Beatles but they were really something special. Even when they arrived, you felt in awe of them. They were so friendly and so funny. We played first, then Tommy Burton, then the Beatles. The whole audience surged forward to get as close as possible to the stage. I remember John Lennon singing 'Twist and Shout.' It took the roof off!"

Released late in 1962 the Beatles' first single — 'Love Me Do' — was struggling its way up the charts when **Joe Regan** was offered the opportunity to book the band. "I'd never heard of them, but the agent said they would be okay and so I said I'd be guided by his judgement." said Joe. "I had them at the **Ritz** on the Sunday evening, but on the Sunday morning their manager, **Brian Epstein** phoned me. 'Joe,' he said, 'Look after my boys. They really are going to be something special.' I arranged for sandwiches and tea to be put in their dressing room and I went in to introduce myself when they arrived. They were really quite charming but I suddenly realised there were only three Beatles present when Brian Epstein had told me they were a four-handed band. 'Don't worry,' they laughed, 'He'll be here in time.' Remembering what I'd promised Brian, I went to the doorman to ask him to keep an eye open for another mop-head. As I spoke, I heard girls screaming and crying. They were pulling this lad out of a taxi by scruff of his neck. It was the missing Beatle. Me and the doorman waded in and fought the girls off. It was total mayhem in York Road that night!"

The Regans also had the band at the **Old Hill Plaza**. **Phil Ackrill** of the **Diplomats** remembers, "Bonfire night was coming up. Before the show we were up on the back roof of the Plaza waving sparklers, and the Beatles came up and joined in. We opened the show and **Denny Laine** played 'Sabre Dance' with the guitar balanced on the back of his neck. The Beatles were behind us, on the revolving stage, dancing around and cheering us. Then we did 'Take Five', a modern jazz piece that has five beats to the bar in its time signature — in other words, it was a nightmare to play. Paul McCartney told Bev that their drummer would never be able to play anything like that. Bev lived off that quote for ages."

With 'Love Me Do' propping up the British top twenty record chart, the Beatles set off to perform their final exhausting stint at the **Star Club**, Hamburg.

Setting off for Hamburg at around the same time was a lad from Coney Green Drive, Longbridge — **Geoff Turton. Chuck Botfield** of the **Rockin' Berries** takes up the story. "**Terry Bond, Tim Munns, Clive Lea** and me were battling on in Germany. Dougie, Dennis and Jimmy had gone home and the band was sounding thin. We got in touch with Geoff Turton, who at the time was strumming with the **Swinging Chimes**, and asked if he fancied throwing in his lot with the Berries."

Geoff, the red haired lad who Chuck had remembered as the clarinet student at Turves Green Schools, didn't need asking twice — by the end of the week he was in Hamburg Rockin' with the Berries.

Chuck continues, "He joined as a backup guitarist to me, to fill out the sound, that was the idea. We were doing loads of Chuck Berry material at the time and I wanted that 'chunk chunk' vamp on the bass strings going while I soloed. As we played one night, I was aware of a fellow at the side of the stage, watching my fingers intently whenever I played a lick. We did 'Roll Over Beethoven' and this fellow asked to see me after the set. It was **George Harrison.** He asked me to show him the guitar break I'd been playing. We sat there, in the dressing

The Rockin' Berries with Chuck Berry himself — the man who inspired their name

room, and I taught him note for note, what I'd played. Twelve months later it appeared as one of most popular tracks on the their second album, 'With The Beatles'.

"There was always a chap around, recording everything," said Chuck, "Maybe that's why Geoff suddenly announced that he wanted to have a go at singing a song. When he told us the song he wanted to do, we nearly had heart failure. It was 'I Remember You', complete with yodel! We were a rhythm and blues band and here we were playing corny country and western! But he did it! He hit the high notes easily, in a pure falsetto and we realised we *had* something."

Into the Berries' set came 'Sherry', a song that was high on the charts. It was by the New York harmony outfit the Four Seasons, and featured the falsetto of Frankie Valli. The lead vocal part presented no problem to Geoff Turton. There was another song going over big with the Hamburg crowds. It was called 'Stay', again by a New York 'doo-wop' outfit, this time the Zodiacs. Their lead vocalist, Maurice Williams, was also way up in the Gods with his pitching. Again, Geoff pitched perfectly. After the disappointment of Jack Goode telling them that they were no different to everyone else out there, the Rockin' Berries now had a unique vocal sound. With Clive Lea's confidence as an impressionist growing, they would set themselves apart from any competition that they were likely to encounter on their return home to Birmingham.

The **Beachcombers,** because of their excellent working relationships with 'name' artistes who were appearing at the Handsworth Plaza, began to attract attention from the London 'in crowd'. Their leader, **Pete Green** had now taken a professional name for himself, **Peter Lee Stirling**, and was being rated not only as a musician and vocalist, but also a songwriter with commercial potential. The band were moving in the right circles, recording demonstration discs at the **Oriole Studios** for an up and coming composer, **Les Reed**.

"We were rubbing shoulders with the stars," sighs Dezi Vyse. "For some reason the band had a weekend off and were due to recommence work at the Plaza on the Monday evening. **Bobby Coral** had been invited to spend the weekend with Helen Shapiro's cousin at the family home in London. We told him not to be late for the Monday gig, and he wasn't. He came running into the Plaza straight from Snow Hill station with a suitcase under his arm. He desperately needed a wash and shave and he laughed as he said, 'Don't worry lads, all my bathroom stuff is in the suitcase.' Then he opened the suitcase and began pulling out bras and panties and skirts! He'd grabbed the wrong suitcase as he got off the train at Snow Hill!"

The Beachcombers

Chapter Eleven

MAYBE TOMORROW A NEW ROMANCE

Carl Wayne and the Vikings had struggled through the snow that blanketed Birmingham, to perform at the **Taboo Club**, Stirchley. It was Saturday night, 5th of January, 1963, and immediately after the show, they set off in their Dormobile for a six month engagement arranged by Rockin'-Berry-turned-agent, **Dougie Thompson**. The destination — a place that was fast becoming the promised land for would-be rock 'n' roll stars — Germany.

In exile, the band were unaware of the Beatles' debut on national TV at the end of the following week. **ATV** transmitted **Thank Your Lucky Stars** from the **Astoria Studios** in Aston and featured the newly released single, 'Please Please Me'. Almost overnight, British pop music took a new direction and the Vikings, miles away in Hamburg for the next six months, would be returning to a changed landscape.

Just as Bill Haley's 'Rock Around the Clock' and the whole Presley package had given such wondrous inspiration to the youth of Britain with its raw energy back in '56, so, seven years later, the sheer energy of the Beatles — with their songs, mostly self-penned; their inovative appearance; their innocent attitude and proud declaration of working class backgrounds — kicked into touch all the stagnant and contrived methods that had previously been applied by show biz moguls. The age old saying 'the public wants what the public gets' was dead and buried for the time being. From now on it was 'the public gets what the public wants', and what the

Carl Wayne & the Vikings

youth of Britain wanted was a shot of rhythm and blues.

In Birmingham, the early months of '63 were producing untold misery as winter lingered on with no end, it seemed, in sight. **Robbie Harper** remembers that bitterly cold winter so well. Robbie was the guitarist with the band, **Dean Wade and the Wademen**. 'Dean' was **Joe Bannon**, a scaffolder from Inkerman Street in Lozells, the other Wademen were **Bruce Gibbons**, **Gary Holder** and **Colin Eaves**. "A furniture retailer, Mr Osborne, heard us. Mr Osborne also owned **Bearwood Ice Rink** and booked us there four nights a week regular. Great! Free skating, the lot! Joe Bannon turned up straight from work one night with a gang of his scaffolding mates. The manager of the rink said something about their bad language, and promptly copped one on the chin! That was the end of the gig for us. So," Rob goes on, "luckily, we were offered six nights a week at the **Dolls Club**, backing the strippers. Being greedy lads we did other bookings first, as we didn't start down the Dolls Club until eleven o'clock. But our van was an old Standard 10 pickup with just canvas sides. There was no heater in the driver's cab anyway. It was way below zero every night for months and we'd be frozen stiff in the back of the truck begging for mercy. We'd play the first set at the Dolls still wearing our balaclavas!"

Maybe **Rodney Wright**, who, with brother **Nigel**, played in the Rednal outfit, the **Eko's**, had warmer climes on his mind as he sat on the sofa with his girlfriend, Diane Lloyd, at her parents' house in Meadvale Road, Rednal.

*Carl Barron & the
Cheetahs on
'For Teenagers Only'*

"Diane had this monkey doll, and she was clothing it with this leopard skin material that she'd bought from the Rag Market," explained Rodney. "I spotted a gimmick," he said, failing to spot the pun, "and I thought that if we bought a load of this cloth and had some suits made from it, we'd be a little different from the rest of herd. It was getting to be a bit of a jungle out there."

Purchase the cloth they did. The seamstress at the Alexander Theatre in John Bright Street made up the costumes that were, in use, 'sweatbuckets'. Danny King, on witnessing the Ekos in their outfits suggested a name change, and one of their first engagements as **Carl Barron and the Cheetahs** was at the **Queen Mary**

Ballroom, in the middle of Dudley Zoo. Everything was fine until the band decided to take some fresh air during the interval and went walkabout around the grounds in their cheetah outfits!

Also sucked into the world of gimmickry were Erdington's **Evergreens**. **Alan Buxton**, their drummer tells the story. "We were playing, of all places, the **Sherwood Rooms**, in Nottingham and during the interval, a London bloke, **Mike West**, introduced himself as a singer who went by the name of **Robby Hood**. He'd had a band of Merry Men, but they'd had enough of forest life and returned to normality as the **Cliftones** (named after Clifton Hall in Rugby, the residence of promoter **Reg Calvert**, their manager). They were all Brummies — **Rod Bainbridge**, **Barry Pritchard** and **Glen Dale**, and shortly after that, they changed names again and became the **Fortunes**. "Any road up," continues Alan, "we were playing at the **Fellowship Hall**, off Sutton Parade, and this Robby Hood bloke turns up and asks us to come in with him. It was a hard decision to make as we were doing well as the Evergreens, but in the end it was the sheer daftness of it all that won us over."

Men in tights — Robby Hood & the Merrimen

'Boots' Grice, Alan Buxton & Nick Stevens

Colourful leather waistcoats were made by Alan's mother. Tights were obtained from a theatrical costumier "up Broad Street, somewhere", and with leather boots from the Rag Market, Alan, along with fellow former Evergreens — **Dave Cole**, **Ed Gateley**, **Nick Stevens**, and **Martin 'Boots' Grice** — began riding through the glen as **Robby Hood's Merrimen**.

"The guitarist would play the open-

ing fanfare from the television theme tune, and Robby Hood would fire an arrow from his bow into a dartboard on the other side of the stage (or at least, that's what he aimed for!) and then make his grand entrance! We must have been raving mad!" chuckled Alan Buxton.

Sober as judges – Pete Oliver, John Singer, Dennis Detheridge, an MU rep & John Gibbins adjudicate at the 1962 Locarno Beat Group Contest while Colin B Tempest & the Buccaneers swash their buckles

Watching the same television shows as the Merrimen, were Halesowen's **Juventors**. Obviously influenced by Robert Shaw's antics on the high seas of Pinewood Studios, they became **Colin B Tempest and the Buccaneers**, the part of Mr Tempest being taken by **Colin Bloomer**. **Mick Jones**'s mother sewed Lurex onto the collars of their new blue jackets, bought from Fosters in Dudley, and in an old ambulance given to them by Mr Williams of the Halesowen Motor Company, the Black Country Buccaneers set sail for Hurst Street, where they hove to at the **Locarno Ballroom** and faired extremely well in the Beat Group Contest. "From then on," said Mick Jones, "we had discounts from Fosters in Dudley because they thought we were 'personalities'!"

The musical instrument retailers weren't complaining about sales figures as young hopefuls from all over Birmingham converged on their premises for guitars and drum kits. The most popular retailers targeted were **George Clay** on Broad Street, alongside the BBC; **Jack Woodroffe** in John Bright Street next to Chetwyn's; **Yardleys** in the Snow Hill arches; **Kay Westworth**, in Cannon Street; and **Jones & Crossland** in Hinckley Street, by **Alex's Pie Stand** pitch. Alex wasn't complaining either. His Snackerie, on the corner of Hill Street, was doing better than ever with the bands meeting up at his catering van in the wee small hours. Bands like **Johnny and the Alpines**, the **Atmospheres**, **Danny Ray and the Rave Ons** with **Mark Raymond**, the **Cordettes**, **Lee Zenith and the Cimarrons**, **Roy Vears and the Strangers**, the **Rotundas**, **Carl Fenn and the Mysteries**, **Mark Time and the Countdowns**, **Lee Stevens and the Satellites**, the **Sombreros** and the **Astonaires** (where did they come from?) could regularly be spotted munching on the Fleur De Lys specials after an evening of 'Walking the Dog.'

*Alex's regulars –
the Rotundas . . .*

Phil Ackrill remembers a Thursday evening prior to Easter when the **Diplomats** were at the pie stand. "We've got to go to London." said **Denny Laine**, so frustrated with provincial life. "That's where it all happens! That's where the deals are made!"

So, the Diplomats finished off their pies, licked their fingers and set off down the M1. Next morning, having spent the night catnapping in their van on a car park at the back of Marble Arch, Denny and his disciples grabbed a quick wash and brush up. Then they went in search of London's Tin Pan Alley only to find the publishers and record companies all closed for the holiday.

*. . . the Sombreros
and the Astonaires*

"It was Good Friday and everywhere was shut!" laughs Phil. "Was fate trying to tell us something?"

Scunthorpe, however, was open when Denny Laine and the Diplomats arrived to perform at the Town's Baths. On arrival, the promoter informed Denny that they were to be joined onstage during their second set by an Elvis type singer, **Nicky James**. "No we ain't!" was Denny's blunt answer. "We're the Diplomats. Full stop!" During the interval the promoter again tried to coax Denny into sharing the limelight. "He's from your neck of the woods — Tipton. Everybody's expecting a few songs from

NICKY JAMES with DENNY LAINE and THE DIPLOMATS
Communications to Ralph Horton Enterprises,
110 Wake Green Road, Birmingham, 13.
Phone: SOUth 4097

him. I've got him on the posters for God's sake!

"Eventually Denny agreed," said Phil Ackrill. "and after Nicky James's performance, Denny couldn't have enough of him. He rated him that much."

In fact, Denny invited Nicky James to come straight back to Brum and start a rock 'n' roll career with the Diplomats. When Nicky James commenced that career, he was made as welcome as the flowers in May. A newspaper review by the well respected journalist **Dennis Detheridge** described him as having "the slur of Elvis, the slouch of Billy Fury and the delivery of Bobby Darin." Praise indeed! But back to Scunthorpe Baths. Phil continues, "We drove Nicky back to his home in Mexborough. He said he had to pick up his belongings. We parked outside this house and he went in for his stuff. He emerged about two minutes later with his worldly belongings. A gold lamé jacket and a silver lamé jacket! Denny took him home to Halcombe Road, Tyseley, and showed Nicky to his mother. 'He's staying with us for a while.' he told his mother. 'No he ain't!' said his Mom, and slammed the door. Nicky had to live in the van for a while."

Unlike Nicky James, **Keith Powell** had a roof over his head and three square meals a day with full use of the cruets. Since his untimely exit from the **Vikings**, Keith had been relaxing at his parents' home in Nesbit Grove, Bordesley Green, dabbling in song writing. His father, Jim, had made contact with a small London publishing company belonging to a struggling song-writer, **Barry Mason**.

"I met with Barry, who liked my efforts, took on the publishing and encouraged me to write more. Then I get a visit from my old mate **Robert Hughes**, the one-time Viking, who had 'retired' to the Birmingham Registry Office. He still held a good position there but he must have got the cramp!" quipped Keith, but failing to get a laugh, "because he wanted to get back into groups. He needed a band and asked me to put one together for him."

This Keith did. He brought in **Mal Ritter** on drums, **Phil Gaynor** on sax, **John Allseybrook** on bass and **Colin Wood** with his prized Guild guitar.

"The 'in' music was rhythm and blues" Keith went on "Ray Charles was a big artiste with the public. His band were called the Raelettes, after him, so I thought '**Bobby Valentine**? Valentine? Yeah, the **Valettes**! What happened? Bobby Valentine did one gig, lost his bottle and 'opped it to Canada, leaving me with a band that I didn't even need!"

Keith Powell & the Valets

With **Mal Ford** and his Bird organ poached from **Pat Wayne's Deltas**, the dance halls and pub function rooms of Birmingham welcomed back Keith Powell with the Valettes. "The only problem we had," said Keith, "was that advertising posters would always bill the band as the Valets and not Valettes. So we settled for **Keith Powell and the Valets**. We may as well have called ourselves Keith Powell and the Car Cleaners!"

Although he wasn't best pleased when Mal left, Pat Wayne acknowledged the need for change. "I also needed something new in my music. A new challenge," said Pat. "I was twenty three and I still had that killer instinct. By chance I met **Brian Sharpe**, of the **Rockin' Jaymen** at **Alex's Pie Stand**. Brian marked my card. Micky, their singer, was leaving. The Jaymen had two wonderful saxes blowing for them in **Monk Finch** and **Dario Capaldi**, who had just returned from the Hamburg stint with **Johnny Neal's Starliners**. They also had a great guitarist, **Jeff Roberts**. What a sound! It was a chance to really sing some good strong powerful stuff. That was it. After six years, as far as I was concerned, the Deltas were grounded."

About to fly like the bird on the sign outside the Golden Eagle, was the **R&B Quartet**. In April '63, the **Winwood** broth-

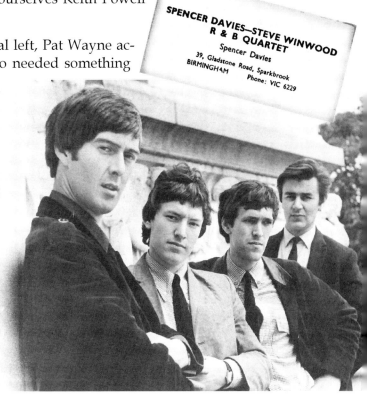

SPENCER DAVIES—STEVE WINWOOD
R & B QUARTET
Spencer Davies
39, Gladstone Road, Sparkbrook
BIRMINGHAM   Phone: VIC 6229

For the boppers — the Jaymen

ers, **Muff** and **Steve** finally boarded the 29a bus that carried them from Kingstanding to the Golden Eagle pub to begin a Wednesday night residency. They had teamed with drummer **Pete York** and guitarist **Spencer Davis**, who was by then teaching at Whittington Oval Primary School. Within two weeks the place was getting packed, but not with dancers, they were further down Hill Street at the **Crown**, bopping to the **Jaymen**. The Rhythm and Blues Quartet's audience, crammed into that upstairs function room, sat enthralled as the boys performed their treatments of songs from the great blues men, Muddy Waters, Howlin' Wolf, John Lee Hooker and Lightnin' Hopkins. The band, *and* the classic material they had chosen were both getting the respect they deserved.

Alan Meredith, of Lennox Street, Lozells believed his strumming days were long over. He'd dabbled in the late fifties with an outfit, the **Cravats**, but when drummer **Roger Grayson** left for the **Dukes**, the Cravats folded.

"It was Spring 1963," says Alan, "and the front door went. They'll pinch anything in Lozells! Anyway, it was this chap, about the same age as me, and he asked if I fancied practising with his band as he'd heard that I used to play. He introduced himself as **Tony Iommi**, a Hank Marvin fanatic whose Mom had a grocer's shop down the road in Park Lane, Aston. We practised at **Burlington Hall Youth Club**, which was almost next to the Orient picture house. The band was the **Pursuers** and the singer used to be able to shake as if he was holding a pneumatic drill! We played at the **Ridgeway Dance Club** on Hockley Hill the following weekend. The poster said 'The **Pursuers** with the Fabulous Shaker!' The band was a bit under the arm to say the least. The drummer would stop half way through a song to light a cigarette. The singer was dreadful — but could he shake!

Alan takes credit for coaxing the young Master Iommi to play lead guitar as opposed to constant strumming. "Strumming was all I could do," says Alan. "I said Tony, 'One of us is gonna have to pick the notes, and I can't do it. But you can!' And could he pick!"

Alan and Tony quit the Pursuers and their machine gunning singer, to search for lads who could actually play and perform to a fair standard. "The Pursuers didn't like it and the singer was shook rigid." Alan sighed, then continued the story. "The first night we went out looking for recruits, we called into the Junction pub in Dartmouth

Street, and got talking, by chance, to a bunch of lads who had a band. I said to Tony, "This is heaven sent!"

The lads were drummer **Pat Pegg**, singer **Noel Morris** (a Dubliner, living in Sparkhill who later changed his name by deed poll to **Neil Cressin**) and bass player **Dave Whaddley** from Aston. Neil Cressin takes up the story. "We arranged a rehearsal at the next pub along Dartmouth Street, The Green Man, 'cause they had a room upstairs. Also we had a lead guitarist, **Johnny Lomas** and a girl singer. We had a rule in the band that no one went near the girl singer. At the end of the first rehearsal, Johnny Lomas left after being upstaged by the sheer brilliance of Tony Iommi's talents on guitar and Alan Meredith took the girl singer home. She broke the rules so we got rid of her!"

As the lads, who named themselves the **Rockin' Chevrolets**, assembled for a second rehearsal, it was nearly their last.

"I never could understand electricity." sighed Neil in his soft Dublin tones. "Tony Iommi passed me a power lead and asked me to plug it in. I'd seen people somehow plug things into light bulb sockets, so I did the same, and bingo, the power came on. We started doing my party-piece — Cliff's 'Dancin' Shoes.' Tony was playing Hank's solo,

The Rockin' Chevrolets — Pat Pegg, Neil Cressin, Toni Iomi, Alan Meredith, & (front) Dave Whaddley wait for the Marlborough to open

note for note, so I began dancing like Cliff Richard. I was holding the mic and swinging my arms. My hand hit Tony's guitar and there was this almighty blue flash around the room. We both got flung over the tables. Me and electricity just don't get on!"

Neil did some more 'live' entertainment when the Rockin' Chevrolets made one of their first appearances. "It was at the **Marlborough** pub, Small Heath." laughs Alan Meredith at the memory. "Neil had got hold of an amplifier from a bloke who, according to Neil, was a genius when it came to equipment. So there's Neil, in his gold lamé jacket, in the back room of the Marlborough, giving his all when flames started leaping out the back of his newly acquired amplifier. The Midland Beat newspaper wrote about the incident. It said, "The Rockin' Chevrolets. The hottest band around!"

Down in London a handsome young man by the name of **Johnny Angel** was being groomed for stardom and was booked to appear on the BBC stand at the trade fair being held at Earls Court. Birmingham's **Beachcombers**, who had acted as backup musicians for him at the **Plaza** and so knew his programme, were also engaged. Johnny Angel wore a red suit, the Beachcombers wore purple and the BBC saw the whole event as a golden opportunity to test out colour television. Hence the Beachcombers became the first band to be transmitted in colour. Tommy Bruce, a successful cockney growler who had charted with the old Fats Waller classic, 'Ain't Misbehavin' three years previously, saw the Beachcombers as an ideal combo to accompany him and the boys agreed, changing their name from Beachcombers to the **Bruisers** in the process. **Dezi Vyse** wasn't so sure and eventually left the band, despite the interest they were beginning to attract from major record companies.

The Redcaps

Ma Regan immediately replaced the now London based Bruisers with a driving rock 'n' roll band from Walsall, the **Redcaps**, led by the **Walker brothers**, **Dave**, who played guitar, and **Mick**, who played bass.

"I remember the Walsall boys very well." said **Joe Regan**. "Could they play!

And that fellow Mick. He was funny. Always had a joke for every occasion."

Indeed the Redcaps had the Plaza crowd bouncing off the walls with their repertoire of driving rock and rhythm and blues. The Isley Brothers belter, 'Shout!', was always the closing song that was guaranteed to storm the place.

Jon Rowlands remembers his introduction to the Plaza, Handsworth, very well. John, from Erdington, had formed an outfit, the **Boll Weevils** with himself, **Billy Dixon**, **Pete Webb** and **Geoff Nichols** making up the personnel.

"We were only kids and we'd played some youth clubs." said John, "We thought we'd go for the big time. Ma Regan auditioned us at her house in Edgbaston and booked us to play the following Saturday at the Plaza supporting a London band that was about to make it big — **Tom Jones and the Squires**. But they never turned up, so the Boll Weevils had to take the stage as the 'big London band'. We'd never faced an audience like the Plaza crowd before. When the compere said, 'From London! The Bollweevils!' the crowd surged forward and a few girls screamed. From there, we went to the **Old Hill Plaza** and then the **Ritz**, all in one night. No one questioned our obvious inexperience. We were as green as grass!"

At the **West End Ballroom**, **Gerry Levene and the Avengers** were performing what he called 'stamping' songs. "This was way before the Dave Clark Five," said Gerry. "We'd be doing 'Do You Love Me,' 'Do You Wanna Dance' and 'Twist and Shout,' stamping our feet to the beat. The audience did the same, as hard as they could on that specially treated dance floor. Mr Lardner, the manager, would be holding his head in his hands!"

For some reason, **John Watson**, a guitarist in the Avengers, decided that he'd had enough and quit. "We advertised in the Mail. The advert read, 'must have a Fender guitar.' and a young lad from Lea Hall had the necessaries. To be honest, it was his enthusiasm that got him the job. He was just full of what it takes to be in a band. He was, of course, **Roy Wood**."

The good news for Senor **El Riot**, of Pype Hayes, was that offers of professional engagements for the band were arriving daily. Engagements that would take them to other parts of the country, to London maybe, or even abroad, to Germany. The bad news was that the **Rebels** didn't share El Riot's enthusiasm.

Brian Betteridge takes up the tale. "**Micky Pinder**, although he wasn't in the Rebels, would sometimes fill in on piano. He'd do things like 'Telstar' when he came with us. Mick, like El (**Ray Thomas**) Riot,

The music is all around you with the...

Clavioline REVERB

Incorporating the World's Finest Reverberation Unit

CAN BE USED TO COMPLEMENT A PIANO OR AS AN INDEPENDENT UNIT ON A PORTABLE STAND

was all for the bright lights. I was looking after my Mom and didn't want to be away on the road. Same as **Bob Sheward**. He was working for his dad as a car mechanic. Perfectly happy around Brum, but turning pro meant leaving everything behind and **John Lodge** was determined to serve his apprenticeship at Parkinson Cowan. So that was it for El Riot and the Rebels. Ray and Mick Pinder formed a band with a couple of other blokes, called themselves the **Krew Kats** and set off for Germany. Mick Pinder borrowed thirty quid off me and bought a *Clavioline*. It was like a little organ that clipped on the front of the piano and gave off weird and wonderful effects like orchestra strings to augment the band. I went over to the Golden Cross on Short Heath, Erdington to join up with the singing dustman himself, **Johnny Carroll** and his group, the **Olympics** which also included **Ron Dickson** and **Steve Price**." Brian paused, closed his eyes and scratched his temples. "Do you know," he said, wagging his finger, "I can't remember getting that thirty quid back."

Danny Burns and the Phantoms were also heading for Germany and the erotic delights of Hamburg's Reeperbahn. "We'd been managed for a while by two car dealers, **John Saint** and **Bruce Jordan**. The work they found us was okay, like the **Reservoir Hotel** at Earlswood, but when **Dougie Thompson** offered us Hamburg, we ripped his arm off. But we needed a guitarist. We'd heard about this lad **Trevor Ireson**, from Whitehouse Street, Aston. He was bursting with enthusiasm and had the talent to back it up, but as he was only fifteen, we had to find somebody else. When we arrived home at the end of '63, I saw him with his own outfit, **Trevor Burton**, as he was calling himself, and the **Everglades**, with his old mate **Keith Smart**, from Victoria Road, on drums."

The Olympics

As Ray Thomas, Micky Pinder and Danny Burns with his Phantoms headed out to Germany, so **Johnny Neal and the Starliners** and the **Rockin' Berries** returned. The Starliners' line up was now Johnny, **Graham Dunnet** on guitar, **Terry Franks** on drums and on Bird organ and bass guitar (played at the same time!) **Ian 'Monk' Mutch**. "Like the Berries," said Johnny, "we'd been away so long and created our own style. **John Singer** became our manager and he was the best as far as I was concerned. It was a great team."

The first engagement the Rockin' Berries played, on arriving home, was the **California** pub, Weoley Castle. **Chuck Botfield** recalls the evening so vividly. "It was a function for the **Birmingham City Supporters Club**, organised by **Jack Bond**, who was the father of our drummer, Terry. We now had brand new amps, mics on boom-stands and echo chambers. The programme we had was far superior to our old set. Now we had Geoff Turton's soaring falsetto voice with harmonies to enhance it, and also Clive Lea's expertise as a front man, throwing in his hilarious impressions. We played the first half to absolute silence and we thought we'd died the proverbial death. Then the roof came in. Without wanting to sound big headed, it dawned on us that we were just so far ahead."

Whilst they had been away Clive's father had been sending demonstration tapes of the band to **Decca**, and the Berries finally received the call they had been waiting for when Decca agreed to record a self penned effort of the Berries, **Wa Wa Woo** coupled with **Rockin' Berries Stomp.**

The evening prior to the session, the Rockin' Berries appeared in Newcastle Upon Tyne and then drove three hundred miles south to Decca in London, where they began recording at ten the following morning. "I was the only one in the band with a driving licence!" laughed Chuck, "I wasn't laughing then!"

Bobby Hill and the Dominators of Copeley Hill, Erdington, were no more. **Greg Masters**, the bass player, set off up Slade Road to the 65 bus terminus to meet up with brothers **Chris** and **Ralph Wheeler**, whose outfit was called the **Dakotas**. Soon after this, with rhythm and blues gaining popularity by the day, they were joined by a howlin' blues singer, **Roy Everett**. With a front man that sounded a *bit* like a famous mountain the band opted to call themselves the **Climbers** in their quest to make it to the top.

Trevor Burton & the Everglades at Allens Cross WMC, Northfield

Roger Hill and **Graham Gallery**, also left over from the defunct Dominators, put in with **Tony Carter** and drummer/ songwriter, **Bugsy Eastwood**, to form the appropriately named **Brumbeats.**

Brumbeat was a term now on everyone's lips and **ATV**, in Aston, couldn't

Miar Davies

help but be aware of it. Their reaction was to devise and broadcast a regular feature for the region. The thirty minute programme, 'For Teenagers Only,' gave Midland viewers a chance to see local artistes in action. Resident on the show was singer **Miar Davies**, a young lady from Redditch, and **Terry with his Senoritas**, although no one ever really figured out where he came from. Guests would be maybe **Steve Brett and the Mavericks**, a country and western band from Wolverhampton, or Brum's very own **Denny Laine and the Diplomats** with their dyed blonde hairstyles, performing their own material like Denny's early effort, 'Forever and a Day'.

Phil Ackrill picks up the story. "We'd done two or three television shows by then and we loved being recognised when we were out and about. One afternoon, myself and **Bev Bevan** were playing football at Daisy Farm Park. **Jasper Davis**, our mate from schooldays was with us, joining in the kick-about. Some girls recognised me and Bev, because of our blonde hair, and gave chase. We ran, but not *too* fast, and we let them catch us up. The girls asked for autographs and we obliged. One of the girls handed her piece of paper to Jasper and asked him to sign it, which he did. When the girls had gone, I asked him what he signed. '**Jasper Carrott** and the Corndreamers' was his reply — and the name has stuck from that day to this."

Chapter Twelve

Gotta Go? Go Now!

In May '63, **Norrie Paramore** would have been seated in his office, studying whatever chart success his artistes had achieved over the period of the last few months. On paper, he should have been dancing around the room. His pride and joy, Cliff Richard, was at that very moment, sitting amongst the top five best selling singles with his recording, 'Lucky Lips' and Columbia's other money-spinner, Frank Ifield, had recently given Mr Paramore yet another number one hit with 'The Wayward Wind'. Norrie Paramore, however, was no fool. He knew that the times they were a-changin'. He needed new acts that had the same vibrancy and enthusiasm as the new faces recently launched by George Martin, the Artists and Repertoire boss of Parlophone. Under Mr Martin's wing were artistes that were reflecting the spirit of the British teenager. On Mr Martin's roster were the Beatles, with their two in-house songsmiths, Lennon and McCartney; Gerry Marsden and the Pacemakers with Gerry's obvious 'teenybopper' appeal; and a handsome young man whose recording, 'Do You Want to Know a Secret', was currently sharing top five honours with Cliff Richard — Billy J Kramer and his excellent band from Manchester, the Dakotas.

Perhaps that is why Norrie Paramore homed in on Birmingham. He needed to combat the so called 'Merseybeat' with something and the term 'Brumbeat' seemed to roll off the tongue. Contact was made with Birmingham entrepreneur, **Bob Smith**, an agent who managed several bands. He rounded up a whole bunch of Brummie outfits to go through their paces for Mr Paramore at the **Moat House Club**, in Moat Row.

"We heard that EMI were making moves to sign some Brummie bands and their talent scouts rated us. We got quite excited at the prospect of being involved." said **Diplomat Phil Ackrill**. "Then we found out that it would be a 'shop window' situation, and **Denny Laine** was having none of that, thank you very much!"

Gerry Levene also declined the chance to audition for Mr Paramore.

"I'd heard he was looking for five or six bands but I was wary of being just one of many," explained Gerry. "**Ma Regan** finally made up my mind for me. She said she'd recommended the **Avengers** and the **Redcaps** to **Decca** and reckoned they were interested."

The **Rockin' Chevrolets** were just one more of a hundred or so bands that were to be ignored by the talent scouts. Not that it bothered them. They were more than happy to turn up at the **Bolton** pub in Small Heath, where they performed every Sunday evening, or the **Shareholders** in Park Lane, Aston, just across from the grocer's shop that **Tony Iommi**'s parents kept.

"We did the opening night of the new lounge at the Shareholders." recalls **Neil Cassin**. "Mrs Iommi organised it. I remember there was an instrumental record out at the time, 'The Cruel Sea' by the Dakotas. Tony played it brilliantly. The crowd went barmy. I used to love going to the Iommi's." Neil continues, "Tony's mom was a lovely lady. She used to ask if I wanted a drop of anything in my tea. Being a Dubliner, how could I refuse?"

Alan Meredith shudders as he recalls an event that nearly finished Tony Iommi as a guitarist. "He had a job in a factory, operating a guillotine and managed to chop off the tips of a couple of fingers on his right hand. Being left handed, those were the fingers that pressed down the guitar strings. It must have been awful for the lad. Playing guitar was his life." Alan's mother apparently gave Tony the initial solution to the problem. "Tony was at our house in Lennox Street, feeling pretty depressed about the whole situation. Mom was sewing and there were a few thimbles lying around. He fitted a couple to his fingers and realised that he could play, using thimbles as substitutes for his fingertips. I think it progressed from there. Tony had caps made especially for him after that."

As **Nicky James**, with **Denny Laine and the Diplomats**, took to the stage at the **Springfield Ballroom**, word was passed to them that **Tony Hatch**, of **Pye Records** was in the room.

"He actually made the journey to Birmingham because he'd heard all about Nicky James," said **Phil Ackrill**. "That's who he came to spy on, but he told us later that although he thought Nicky was a great singer with a great image, he was too 'Elvis'."

It was Denny Laine's voice that Tony latched onto (even though Denny had a dreadful cold that evening) and the fact that the band were into performing their own material. As a result of his visit to the Springfield Ballroom, Tony Hatch summoned Denny Laine and the Diplomats to his London recording studio where they cut Denny's own original song, 'Forever and a Day'. Now all the boys had to do was to return to Birmingham and wait for a release date.

As the Diplomats waited, in early June, '63, so Norrie Paramore and his assistant **Bob Barratt** were being escorted by **Bob Smith** (acting as guide and interpreter) through the magical mayhem of the Bull Ring. They strolled past the old fish market steps and the little old blind lady selling carrier bags. Then, weaving around the hand-carts left haphazardly at the foot of Nelson's statue, they crossed Edgbaston Street and, after wading through the cabbage leaves that littered the pavement, the party arrived at the steps of the **Moat House Club**. Inside, Messrs Paramore and Barratt spent the entire day listening to the thirteen outfits that Bob Smith had recommended as worthy of a hearing. Eight bands were unceremoniously crossed off the list as the day wore on. The smiling survivors were: **Pat Wayne and the Rockin' Jaymen**, **Danny King and the Royals**, **Carl Barron and the Cheetahs**, **Keith Powell and the Valets**, and **Mike Sheridan and the Nightriders**. From now on, when promoters displayed posters advertising their forthcoming shows, the names of these star Brumbeat attractions would be followed by the words — *'Columbia Recording Artistes'*.

Five very happy bands outside the Moat House with Norrie Paramore

Confidence in Brumbeat grew further when **Decca** released a second single by the **Rockin' Berries**, entitled 'Itty Bitty Pieces', and the **Bruisers** debut record, 'Blue Girl', was released on **EMI**'s **Parlophone** label.

Pat Wayne's first recording for **Columbia** was 'Go Back to Daddy', written by **John Chesterton** and **Bob McNally** (two progress chasers from the Rover, Solihull). It was a strong rock number, but the song-pluggers immediately realised that the name **Jaymen** was a little too close for comfort to 'Peter Jay and the Jaywalkers', the East Anglian outfit signed to Decca.

"Someone at Columbia thought **Beachcombers** was a good name," Pat explained, "So I sought out **Peter Lee Stirling** and **Bobby Coral**, who had traded as the Beachcombers prior to their association with **Tommy Bruce**, and got their permission to use the name. We were always credited on record as Pat Wayne *with* the Beachcombers, because Norrie Paramore thought the band had the potential to record in their own right, which indeed they did, releasing an instrumental single, 'Mad Goose'."

Pat Wayne & the Beachcombers meet Stanley Mathews at the Victoria Football Ground, Stoke on Trent

Keith Powell and the Valets' first recording was also a lively piece,

'Come On and Join the Party', which received healthy radio play. "Because I'd written the song," said Keith, "I told Norrie about the contract I had with **Barry Mason**'s publishing company. **EMI** bought up my contract which released me from Barry. Four years later and Barry's writing million sellers like 'The Last Waltz', 'Everybody Knows' and 'Les Bicyclettes de Belsize'!

"I was still working at Cadbury's," laughs **Mal Ford** of the **Valets**. "and our record would come on the wireless during the lunch break. I'd be strolling round the canteen with my dinner on the tray, pretending I couldn't hear it."

The Cheetahs don civvies to meet boxer Johnny Prescott

The first offering by **Carl Barron and the Cheetahs** was the appropriately named 'This is Only the Beginning'. Unfortunately, it was also the end as far as EMI were concerned as **Colin Smith** alias Carl Barron packed his bags and left for South Africa following a row with his wife, although he wisely left the cheetah suit out of his case.

For **Mike Sheridan and the Nightriders**, their first pitch at the charts was 'Tell Me What We Gonna Do'. What Bob Smith *did* do, to create interest, was issue a press release informing the nation that Mike Sheridan and the Nightriders were to play support to Frank Sinatra at the Sands Hotel, Las Vegas, for a fee of twenty five thousand pounds!

"It was alright for Bob Smith, tucked away in his office," sighed Mike, "but we still had to turn up at our bookings. We'd be at the **Rainbow Suite**, over the Co-Op in Dale End and the audience would be singing 'High Hopes' as we walked onto the stage!"

"I hated both of my records." said **Danny King**. 'Tossin' and Turnin'' and 'Young Blood' just weren't my idea of songs, but that's what EMI dictated would go out. And they never used my band, the **Royals**. They always insisted that the **Nightriders** backed me on record."

A band who missed out on the Moat House showcase were the Cyclones — **Chalky Marsh**, **Pete Dawson**, **Phil Riches**, **Bunny Robinson** and their newly acquired vocalist, **Mark Raymond**.

Mark (**Ken Hoban** to his Mom) picks up the tale. "I telephoned **Bob Smith** and asked what the chances were of making a record for Co-

lumbia. As luck would have it, **Bob Barratt** was in town. We met him at the **Crown** in Hill Street, and played him some of our songs. It seemed one minute we were kids, saving up to buy a record, next minute, we're at **EMI**'s **Abbey Road Studios**, making our own record."

Once more the song pluggers pointed out possible problems over the band's name as there was an American outfit also called the Cyclones, so the boys became **Mark Raymond and the Crowd** for their one and only release — 'Girls'.

Mark Raymond & the Crowd

Gerry Levene & the Avengers

Ma **Regan**'s remark to **Gerry Levene** concerning **Decca**'s interest was true. The Decca men came to the **West End Ballroom** and 'did the deal' with the **Avengers**. The Decca men then motored through Hockley and into Handsworth, where, at the Plaza, they also 'did the deal' with the **Redcaps**. The Walsall boys' barnstormer 'Shout' was chosen as their debut single, while Gerry Levene and the Avengers' first release was to be 'Doctor Feelgood'.

Keith Powell makes his point. "Okay, none of us were charting, but we were in there with the big boys. Most of us were doing major television shows that were networked across the country to millions of viewers. Shows like **Thank Your Lucky Stars** featured the Brum bands regularly. Consequently our standards improved. All the time we were making progress. It was just that Britain was so Mersey Beat mad at the time."

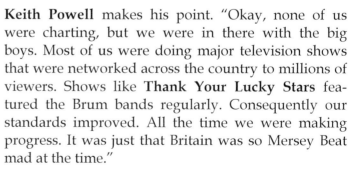

Pat **Wayne and the Beachcombers** were summoned to **Abbey Road Studios** where **Norrie Paramore** thrust a record in to their hands. He told them to learn the arrangement as they would start recording in one hour's time. "It was the Beatles' version of 'Roll Over Beethoven', as yet, unreleased." said Pat. "**Jeff Roberts** studied the guitar part and I quickly got the lyrics." It was the same guitar riff that **Chuck Botfield** had laboriously shown to George Harrison twelve months previously in a Hamburg night club. With the tape turning, the Beachcombers, with saxes blowing like a hurricane, cut a blistering version of the Chuck Berry classic.

A record signing at Lewis's with Keith Powell & Billie Davis

Thirty five years later, the producer of that record, **Bob Barratt**, still finds it hard to understand why the record was never a hit. "We sold eighty odd thousand copies," said Bob. "On today's figures, you'd be number one for the rest of the year."

"Everyone remembers where they were on the evening of Friday, 22nd of November, 1963" said **Greg Masters**. "I had recently joined the **Nightriders**, replacing **Brian Cope** on bass and we'd spent all day at **Abbey Road Studios** recording 'Please Mr Postman'. We came out, marched over the zebra crossing that is so famous now, and as we walked to the tube we saw the newspaper hoardings, '*Kennedy assassinated*'."

E arly in '64, **Ray Thomas** and **Mick Pinder** were back in Birmingham following their stint in Germany as the **Krew Kats**. "I was at the bus stop in Corporation Street," said **Brian Betteridge**. "I looked up and saw Ray. He was tired and skint but said that he and Mick Pinder were in the market for some blokes to start up a new band. They were giving it one more go."

Gerry Day & the Dukes

Clint Warwick gives his recollection of events. "Rhythm and Blues was the stuff to play. I'd left **Gerry Day's Dukes** and teamed up again with **Danny King**. **Denny Laine** had also expressed his wish to be a part of a new project so we started rehearsing with **Graeme Edge** from the **Avengers**. We'd planned to call ourselves the **R&B Preachers**, but a chance meeting at the **Moat**

House with Mick Pinder and Ray Thomas changed everything."

Danny King's interest in the new venture had waned and Messrs Thomas and Pinder had been approached by **Phil Myatt** to put a band together with a view to sponsorship coming from local brewers, **Mitchells and Butlers**.

"We even went as far as having the **M&B Five** painted on the side of our van," said Clint. "The bloke from M&B came to a rehearsal — heard us — and promptly dropped the idea! But we knew we had something. It was just a matter of ironing out the creases."

Steve Horton recalls, "We finally got the call from **Pye** that **Tony Hatch** was only budgeted to work with one band. It was either the **Diplomats** or the **Searchers**. Tony Hatch chose the Searchers. History shows that he chose wisely!"

The M&B Five provided Denny with a new challenge when he joined them full-time late in March '64, but with brewery sponsorship out of the window, the boys saw no reason to continue to giving M&B free advertising. "One of us took the 'B' and changed it to Blues. The 'moody' look seemed appropriate, so we kept the initials, and became the **Moody Blues**, simple as that," said Clint Warwick.

The Moodies very first appearance was at the **Carlton**, Erdington, which they'd used as a daytime rehearsal room, much to the annoyance of Sid Reynolds, the manager of Brooks Brothers, the gentlemens' outfitters on the ground floor. By coincidence on that debut performance, the Moody Blues shared the bill with a revamped Diplomats line up that had **Jim Onslow** and **Sprike Hopkins** in as a two-man replacement for Denny Laine.

In April '64, **Chris Blackwell** (proprietor of **Island Records**, a label specialising in West Indian music) was in Birmingham. He had come to take a peep at **Carl Wayne and the Vikings**, but picked up the vibes coming from the **Whisky a Go-Go**, a rhythm and blues club operating from premises above Chetwyn's gents outfitters in Navigation Street. Until the explosion of interest in black music, it had served as the Laura Dixon Dance Studio, where the shy and inhibited were able to shed their frustrations by learning to cha-cha and paso doble to Edmundo Ross records. Hardly a hint of the venue's sedate history remained as Mr Blackwell climbed the stairs to join the enraptured audience. Just one hearing of **Stevie Winwood**'s rendition of 'Georgia On My Mind' was enough for Chris Blackwell's ears, and the **Spencer Davis Group** were signed to Island Records. Their first single, 'I Can't Stand It' (released under licence by **Fontana**, as were all their subsequent records) made the top fifty in November.

The Modernaires at the Tyburn House celebrating the release of their first single

Not to be outdone, the **Modernaires** became the first British act to be signed to the American label **RCA**, and to promote their recording of 'Something On My Mind', they appeared on quite a few national television shows. "But it was really hard work," said **Micky Bakewell**, the vocalist with the Modernaires. "To be successful in the pop world, you have to give it one hundred and ten per cent, and we couldn't go the extra ten per cent. We never turned professional. For us, it wasn't the be and end-all. We were happy in Birmingham."

Joe Regan says the Modernaires had every reason to be happy in Birmingham. "They never stopped working. I had the **Animals** at the **Ritz** when they were number one with 'House of the Rising Sun'. **Eric Burdon**, their singer, asked me who owned the flash cars that were parked in York Road. I had to tell him they all belonged to the Modernaires!"

A call from **Dougie Thompson** to **Piccadilly Records** brought their head of Artists and Repertoire, **John Schroeder**, to **Cadbury's Club**, in Bournville, to view the **Rockin' Berries**. Their unique vocal sound impressed Mr Schroeder so much that the Berries found themselves in the nation's top fifty in late September, '64 with a quaint ditty, 'I Didn't Mean To Hurt You'. As national popularity grew, they appeared at the hip **Marquee Club**, in London's Soho. In the audience was the trouser-splitting singer, P J Proby, and with him was a fellow American, the legendary song plugger, Kim Fowley. Knocked out by the falsetto abilities of Geoff Turton, Kim informed the Berries that he had just the song that would put them in the top ten. The song, written by Carole King and Jerry Goffin had enjoyed some success in the States by the Tokens and was entitled 'He's in Town'.

When John Schroeder heard 'He's in Town', the following morning, he felt the same, and within forty-eight hours, the Rockin' Berries had recorded the song that would, in mid October, '64, make number three on the British hit parade.

Carter & Lewis in their first London bedsit, and at the piano with their manager, Terry Kennedy

John Shakespeare and **Ken Hawker** were a song writing team. Both born and raised in Small Heath, they first met up at Waverley Grammar School. On entering the big wide world, John trained as a metallurgist, and Ken worked in local government, but in 1959 they abandoned Small Heath's aroma of Wimbush bread, for the coffee and doughnut smells of London's Tin Pan Alley to try to chisel out careers as tunesmiths. Turning professional meant that they had to indulge in the obligatory name tinkering. John became **John Carter** and Ken became **Ken Lewis**. The change of names brought a change of luck and Southern Music contracted them as writers. As performers, they were **Carter Lewis and the Southerners** and enjoyed minor success with their first recording, 'Your Momma's Outa Town'. Three years on, and with their recording engineer, **Perry Ford**, joining them, they became the **Ivy League**. Their first release failed, so they went all out to write themselves a hit song, and came up with 'Funny How Love Can Be'.

"The Ivy League, had the same producer as the Berries," explains songwriter John Carter. "Consequently, John Schroeder had access to our catalogue of material and recorded 'Funny How Love Can Be' with the Berries, to be their all important follow-up to 'He's in Town'. Ken Lewis and I pleaded with him to release our version of the song instead. Fortunately for us, John Schroeder did just that, giving us, as writers and performers, our first top ten success."

The **Moody Blues** had by now, gained themselves a London based manager that burned with the same ambitions as them. **Tony Secunda** went to work and set up a recording contract for them with **Decca**. Their first effort, 'Steal Your Heart Away' didn't steal many hearts, but their next recording would shoot them high into the rock 'n' roll hierarchy. It was, of course, 'Go Now', a cover of a Bessie Banks song that the Moody Blues recorded in an unfinished studio at the rear of the Marquee club. In December '64, Messrs **Laine, Edge, Thomas, Pinder** and **Warwick** found themselves not only at the top of the Nation's charts, but in the American top ten as well.

Mr Schroeder did redeem himself with the **Rockin' Berries** when he found them a song by an American band — the Reflections. 'Poor Man's Son' made number five on the national chart in May '65. Just as the record reached the top ten, bass player **Roy Austin** left the band. He was replaced by **Bobby Thomson**, a Liverpool 'whacka' who had once been a member of Merseyside's legendary **Rory Storm and the Hurricanes**, with one **Richard Starkey** on drums.

The sheer hard work that the Berries had put into their careers was rewarded when they were invited to participate in the 1967 **Royal Command Performance**, before Her Majesty, Queen Elizabeth and Prince Philip, Duke Of Edinburgh.

"We're hangin' around at rehearsals," says Bobby Thomson in his Scouse tones, "and **Bob Hope** wanders over and asks if our dressing room is okay. I told him we were sharing with the Ukrainian dancers, and there was about forty of them. He said, '*You've* got problems. I'm sharing with **Harry Secombe, Tom Jones** and **Tanya the Elephant**'. As we were talking, so Tanya stood up and opened the window with her trunk!"

Bobby Thomson gets his breath back and continues. "After the show, we're in line to meet the Royal party. **Clive Lea**, our impressionist, is first, then me. So the Queen, as she shakes Clive's hand, nods to Philip and says, 'He's a good taker offerer, isn't he!' "

Certified — Bobby Thomson

Being a member of the Birmingham in-crowd of the mid-sixties meant regular attendance at **Eddie Fewtrell's Cedar Club**, on Constitution Hill, just up from Bond Street. Waiting to pounce on innocent strangers would be the character of all characters, **'Ready Steady' Teddy**. As the innocent stranger engaged the barmaid for

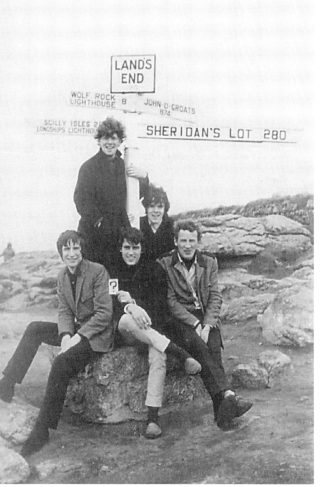

Cedar Club regulars, Sheridan's lot – Mike surrounded by Nightriders – Dave Prichard, Roger Spencer, Roy Wood & Greg Masters

service, so Teddy would tap the stranger on the shoulder and utter his immortal introduction, "Our mom says, can you get me an Export." The Export in question was an upmarket bottled light ale brewed by Mitchells and Butlers which the Cedar Club retailed for five shillings! At around midnight, the featured band, be it **Carl Wayne and the Vikings**, **Danny King and the Mayfair Set** or perhaps **Mike Sheridan and the Nightriders**, who now had **Roy Wood** as their lead guitarist, would call upon **Ready Steady Teddy** to take the stage. Ambling on in his well worn monkey suit and white shirt with its grubby collar and fraying cuffs, Teddy would suddenly acquire a Las Vegas accent as he took hold of the microphone.

"I'm gonna perform a song by my great friend, Tom Jones!" he would drawl as the band played the intro to 'It's Not Unusual'. It was never unusual for Teddy to fail to pitch the key and the whole routine would end in chaos. Order could only be restored by guest musicians taking the stage to play a few of the old 'rockers'. On one occasion the impromptu line up was **Trevor Burton** from the **Mayfair Set**, **Roy Wood** from the **Nightriders**, and **Carl Wayne**, **Bev Bevan** and **Ace Kefford** from the **Vikings**. Here began the **Move**. A move that would, over the next six years, produce ten smash hit singles, all written by Roy Wood.

Johnny Carroll, the singing dustman, hung up his rock 'n' roll shoes in '67, to become a professional comedian. Winning the television talent show **New Faces** in the early seventies, he soon became a nationally known face on Granada Television's Comedians series. **Peter Lee Stirling**, well established as a jobbing songwriter for such artistes as the **Merseybeats** and **Kathy Kirby**, went on to chart success in the early seventies as **Daniel Boone**, with a 'weepy' entitled 'Daddy Don't You Walk So Fast', and then with his own song 'Beautiful Sunday'. His colleague from the **Bruisers**, **Bobby Coral**, in the late '60s, became a member of the **Ivy League**, replacing **John Carter** on stage appearances.

The lad from Cato Street, **Johnny Killigrew**, made it to Nashville, Tennessee in the mid-seventies. Save for a period with **Mick Pinder's Tuxedos**, he had never stayed long with a band. **Greg Masters** was probably right when he said Johnny was too far ahead of everyone to settle. In Nashville he cut a solo album. Sales weren't too healthy, but the most popular track was, undoubtedly, Johnny's stunning version of 'Go Now'. Back in Birmingham late in 1978, while returning from an engagement at the **Opposite Lock** in Gas Street, he was involved in a road accident. Sadly, Johnny Killigrew died as a result of the injuries he sustained.

In December '65, the **Spencer Davis Group** set the nation alive with the Jackie Edwards song, 'Keep on Runnin'', the arrangement layered **Stevie Winwood**'s harsh vocal delivery with mind-blowing distortion on both lead and bass guitars. Twelve months later, the whole world jumped to the hard, pulsating rhythms of **Pete York**'s drumming, as he and **Muff Winwood**, with an octaved bass line, provided the perfect padding for Stevie's stabbing chords on the Hammond organ and his screaming vocals on 'Gimme Some Lovin''.

Tony Iommi, in the mid sixties, had an outfit, the **Rest**, with drummer **Bill Ward**. Towards the end of the decade, and seeking fresh horizons, the two 'airy Astonites answered an advertisement in the publication **Midland Beat** that read '*Ozzie Zig requires gig*'. That's how the extremely shy and reserved vocalist **John 'Ozzie' Osborne**, from Lodge Road, Witton (who had previously been in the **Rare Breed**, and actually had his own microphone) teamed with Tony and Bill. On bass, **Terry 'Geezer' Butler** was brought in to complete the line up and give Aston **Polka Tulk**, possibly the first band to be named after a Pakistani clothing store. Changing their name to **Earth** soon after the launch, the lads set upon a musical trail that would take them to audiences that were termed 'underground'. Determined to make it big they began writing their own material; songs that would set them apart from other hairy hopefuls; and enable them to move to pastures where they would not be awakened by the sound of the Joseph Lucas 'bull' siren. Influenced by the work of author Dennis Wheatley, dark, menacing songs began to appear in their repertoire. One such song was entitled **Black Sabbath**. They re-named the band after that song, and quickly became a mighty force on the powerful underground scene. With Ozzie's screaming vocals, delivering lyrics that were quite often interpreted as messages from the 'other side'; Bill's pounding, driving drumming; Geezer's Tommy gun style of bass playing and Tony's stunning guitar breaks; Black Sabbath taught to the world exactly how heavy metal rock music should be composed and delivered.

The **Moody Blues**, in the mid-sixties, hiccuped in as much as they failed to follow up the huge success of 'Go Now'. The frustration caused by the problem resulted in **Denny Laine** and **Clint Warwick**'s departure from the line up. "We just couldn't find a suitable song," admitted Clint. "We were being handled by **Brian Epstein** and we were right in the thick of the Beatles' circle. In '66 when we were touring with them, Paul gathered us around his piano one afternoon and played us a song that he believed would put the Moody Blues back in the charts."

The song that McCartney had in mind for the Moodies was an old folk song that he had heard in a New York club being performed by an outfit called the Limelighters. It had an 'umpah' feel to it with a bierkeller type sing-a-long chorus.

"We didn't take up Paul's advice," sighed Clint. "I liked it but the others turned it down flat. The song was 'Those Were the Days' and two years later it was a world wide smash for Mary Hopkin. For me it was sudden death. I left the Moodies straight after our season with **Wilson Pickett** in New York. That was on the Friday evening. By the Monday morning I was at a bus stop in Brum with a bag of tools under my arm."

Into the Moody Blues from Swindon, came songwriter and guitarist, **Justin Hayward**, and the former **El Riot** man, **John Lodge**. John had completed his apprenticeship and, on his path to the Moodies, joined **Brian Yeates**, alias **Mark Stuart** in the **Bulldog Breed**.

"Always Mr Supercool was John," says Brian. "We were in Germany and our living quarters were actually backstage of the club. One night, we finished and went to bed. The owner of the club woke us up at four in the morning to play another set. We all dressed and made it to the stage. John Lodge emerged still in his pyjamas, but wearing his sunglasses!"

Shades or no shades, the international success the Moody Blues enjoyed, could never be have been denied them. The creativity in their song writing and their imaginative arrangements were simply world class.

Denny Laine returned to the fore in the early seventies, when he renewed his connections with Paul McCartney and became a member of **Wings**.

When **Roy Wood** quit the **Nightriders** for the **Move** in '66, his position was filled by the guitarist that **Carl Wayne** and company had left behind — **Johnny Mann**. Shortly after this, **Mike Sheridan**, a little disillusioned, took some time out of the business (to build up, as he put it, "a 'tater round") leaving the remaining four Nightriders to become the **Idle Race**. Johnny Mann himself soon departed, and into his shoes stepped a young Shard End lad whose musical career had begun in an outfit called the **Andicaps** — **Jeff Lynne**. The Idle Race, with Jeff's unique approach to song writing, soon became the darlings of the college circuit until '69, when Jeff left to replace Carl Wayne in the Move. The vocal vacancy in the Idle Race was filled by one-time **Dominette, Steve Gibbons**.

Steve, as Mel Lees had predicted, never did subscribe to the shiny suit brigade. By the mid-sixties he had turned the Dominettes into the rebellious **Uglies**; and the Idle Race, by '77, had evolved into the **Steve Gibbons Band**. Steve finally made the charts that year with a hard hitting rendition of Chuck Berry's 'Tulane'.

The Uglies

The amalgamation of the creative talents of Roy Wood and Jeff Lynne produced a chemistry that was electrifying to say the least, and with Bev Bevan seated at the drum kit, they went on, in '72, to shine as the **Electric Light Orchestra**. Roy Wood, however, soon departed to scale new heights with **Wizard**. His zany new project clocked-up two number one hits before its first birthday! Jeff Lynne continued to write the haunting songs, and mastermind the spine-tingling productions of ELO. Over the following ten years they would be acclaimed as one of the greatest bands in the world.

*On Broad Street –
Danny King, Terry
Wallace, Dave Prichard,
Rob Nicholls, Greg
Masters, Trevor Burton,
Gerry Levene & Keith
Smart, still getting their
kicks on the A456*

Of the hundreds of musicians who contributed to the early years of rock in Brum, only a handful, the chosen few, made it to the dizzy heights of the world stage. But each and every one of those who were left behind, either contented with their memories, or to continue performing in the pubs and clubs around the city and beyond, must feel immense pride in their contribution and its legacy. For just as a motorcar from the production lines of Longbridge or Solihull; a high precision rifle from Webley and Scott; or simply a box of the world's favourite chocolates from the Cadbury factory at Bournville; so the haunting melody of the Moody Blues' 'Nights in White Satin'; the blatant aggression of Black Sabbath's 'Paranoid'; or the pleading lyric of the Electric Light Orchestra's 'Telephone Line', all share one common connection — they all carry a hallmark that bears the legend — ***Made in Birmingham.***

PEOPLE

CHEETAHS 100 115 117
CHEQUERS 50
CHESTERTON John 116
CIMARRONS 103
CLARE Wilf 14 15 27 72
CLARKE Vick 61
CLAY George 103
CLIFF ANGEL & THE VIRTUES 47
CLIFTONES 101
CLIMBERS 111
CLIVE & THE DOMINATORS 89
CLIVE LEA & THE PHANTOMS 43 49 63
COLE Dave 61 101
COLIN B TEMPEST & THE BUCCANEERS 102
COLLINS Jill 21
COMETS 8
COMPTON Alan 29
CONGRESSMEN 41
COPE Brian 34 119
COPE Mick 13 29
CORAL Bobby 79 98 116 125
CORDETTES 103
CORSAIRS 15 23 60
COUNTDOWNS 103
COUNTS 51
COUSINS Jimmy 8
COX Alan 50
CRAVATS 106
CRAVEN Mickey 65
CRESSIN Neil 107
CRESTAS 83 85 92
CRICKETS 24
CROWD 118
CRUSADERS 33
CURLEY Pat 19
CUSHERI Joe 35
CYCLONES 118
DAKOTAS 35 36 37 44 50 111
DALE Glen 101
DALE Jim 22
DALLAS Tommy 50
DANCOCK Bill 68
DANIELS Billy 11
DANNY BURNS & THE PHANTOMS 36 93 110
DANNY KING & THE DUKES 18 19 33 39 52 60
DANNY KING & THE MAYFAIR SET 124
DANNY KING & THE ROYALS 60 63 75 94 115
DAVIES Miar 112
DAVIS Billie 59 119
DAVIS Bob 85 112
DAVIS Spencer 91 106
DAWSON Pete 118
DAY Barney 75
DAY Gerry 42 60 119
DAY Kenny 8 11
DEAN Johnny 58 86
DEAN WADE & THE WADEMEN 100

DEELEY Cliff 8
DELTAS 19 20 22 29 37 41 46 58 105
DENNY LAINE & THE DIPLOMATS 86 103 112 114
DETHERIDGE Dennis 10 104
DETHERIDGE Tex 10 11 29 50
DETOURS 50 73
DIAMONDS 83 92
DICKSON Ron 110
DIPLOMATS 86 89 96 103 112 114 120
DIXON Billy 109
DOMINATORS 58 61 76 86 89
DOMINETTES 40 50 64 74 84 127
DONEGAN Lonnie 16 63
DORMAN Don 39 43
DORSEY Warren 8
DOUGLAS Alex 57
DUKES 18 33 39 52 60 106 119
DUNNET Graham 110
EARL Bobby 51
EARTH 125
EASTWOOD Bugsy 111
EAVES Colin 100
ECCLES Albert 12 17
ECKHORN Peter 75
EDGE Graeme 51 119
EDWARDS Archie 14 83
EDWARDS Fred 8
EDWARDS Jackie 125
EKO'S 73 100
El RIOT & THE REBELS 44 45 54 62 63 76 91 109
ELECTRIC LIGHT ORCHESTRA 127
ELSON Josie 32
ELSON Tony 29 31 34 35 36 37 58
ERNIE LANE DANCE BAND 40
EVANS Paul 29 70
EVERETT Roy 111
EVERGLADES 110 111
EVERGREENS 61 101
EXCELSIOR JAZZ BAND 91
FALCONS 82
FENN Carl 62 103
FEWTRELL Eddie 84 123
FINCH Monk 105
FINISTER Tony 39 42
FINN Gary 84
FINN Martin 84
FINN Micky 84
FITZPATRICK Timothy 42
FIVE CARDS 22
FLEETWOOD MAC 45
FORD Mal 41 46 50 105 117
FORD Perry 122
FORRESTER Dean 62
FORTNAM Colin 35
FORTUNES 101
FOWLEY Kim 122
FOXALL Eric 30

FRANKIE & THE HI CARDS 14
FRANKS Terry 110
FRED BRINLOW'S BAND 59
G MEN 71
GALLERY Graham 61 111
GALLON Ken 82
GARNET Tony 27
GATELEY Ed 61 101
GATORS 10 11 13
GAUNTLET Olive 21
GAUNTLET Sonny 22
GAYNOR Phil 105
GERRY DAYS DUKES 119
GERRY LEVENE & THE AVENGERS 47 48 59 85 109
GIBBINS John 102
GIBBONS Bruce 100
GIBBONS Steve 50 54 55 64 74 80 84 127
GIBBS Micky see LEVENE Gerry
GLADIATORS 14 15 72
GOODALL Henry 8
GOODE Jack 33 81 88
GORDON Noele 12
GRASSHOPPERS 30 39 42 43 65 95
GRAYSON Roger 106
GREEN Pete 48 55 68 98
GRICE Martin 'Boots' 62 101
GRIFFITHS Max 'the Nub' 34 92
GROVES Maurice 'Moss' 28 80
HALEY Bill 8
HALL Tony 33
HAMILTON Malc 35
HANCOX Alan 12 17 40
HANCOX Brian 17 40
HARBOR Barry 70
HARPER Robbie 23 100
HARPER Steve 23
HARRIS Johnny 15
HARRIS Micky 72 83
HARVEY Grant 31
HATCH Tony 114 120
HATCHETS 22 50
HAWK Tommy 22 50
HAWKER Ken 122
HAWKES Sid 22 50
HAWKINS Al 40 52
HAWKINS Don 62
HAWKINS Edie 40
HAWKS 72 83
HAYWARD Justin 126
HEADLEY WARD ORCHESTRA 8 11
HEADLEY WARD TRIO 11
HENNEY Jimmy 33
HERD Micky 54
HEWITT Paul 48 64 73 77
HI CARDS 14
HILL Bobby 61 76 111
HILL Roger 61 76 111

HINES Brian 33 35 57 58 86
HINGLEY Alan 15 23
HOBAN Mark (Ken) 31 118
HOBSON Fred 43
HODGKINSON Johnny 15
HOFFMAN TWINS 54
HOLDEN Jimmy 40 74
HOLDER Gary 100
HOLEN Jim 54
HOLLIS Graham 94
HOLLY Buddy 25
HOOD Robby 101
HOPKINS Sprike 47 120
HORDEN Keith 15
HORDEN Ken 15
HORTON Steve 89 120
HOUN'DOGS 14 23 24 27 34
HOWARD Pat 12
HUGHES Robert 40 41 104
HUGHES Ron 13
HULME Colin 8
HUMPHRIES Ray 24 35
HUNTLEY Bill 64
HUSTHWAITE Dave 19 40 41
HUSTHWAITE John 40
IDLE RACE 127
IOMMI Tony 106 114 125
IRESON Trevor 110
IVY LEAGUE 122 125
JAEGER Alan 14
JAMES Nicky 103 114
JASPER CARROTT & THE CORNDREAMERS 112
JAY Jack 70
JAY Peter 70
JAYMEN 52 57 70 106 116
JAYWALKERS 70
JCS PRODUCTIONS 52
JENKINS George 19
JERRY ALLEN & HIS TRIO 12 91
JOHNNY & THE ALPINES 103
JOHNNY KING & THE DIAMONDS 83
JOHNNY NEAL & THE HOUN'DOGS 14 34
JOHNNY NEAL & THE STARLINERS 85 105 110
JOHNNY SHANE & THE ROCKIN' SOLITAIRES 81
JOHNNY WHITEHOUSE & THE CONGRESSMEN 41
JOHNSON Alan 'Big Al' 93
JOHNSON Mark 49
JOLLY Johnny 29
JONES Malc 'the Bones' 24
JONES Maurice 'Mo' 27
JONES Mick 68 102
JONES Reg 51
JONES Tom 109
JONES Viv 39
JORDAN Bruce 110
JUVENTORS 68 102
KEFFORD Chris 'Ace' 51 124

KEITH POWELL & THE JAYMEN 52
KEITH POWELL & THE VALETS 105 115 116
KEITH POWELL & THE VIKINGS 53
KILLIGREW Johnny 61 125
KING Billy 34 93
KING Danny 17 18 33 39 44 52 60 63 75 94 115 117 119 124 128
KING Johnny 83 92
KIRBY John 70
KNIGHT Pete 43 59 64
KNOWLES Tom 92
KREW KATS 110 119
LAINE Denny 86 89 96 103 112 113 114 119 126
LAINE Sonny 90
LANE Ernie 27 40
LARDNER Eric 59
LEA Clive 42 43 49 52 59 63 64 77 88 96 123
LEE STEVENS & THE SATELLLITES 103
LEE ZENITH & THE CIMARRONS 103
LEES Mel 28 42 53 54 65 74 127
LEVENE Gerry 47 48 51 59 85 95 109 113 118 128
LEVIS Carroll 12 13
LEWIS Bill 42
LEWIS Ken 122
LEWIS Smiley 10
LITTLE JIMMY 54
LOCKE Joseph 27
LODGE John 44 54 110 126
LOMAS Johnny 107
LOMBARD Lee 8
LOWE Kenny 81
LUCKMAN Tony 13
LYNNE Jeff 127
LYNTON Jackie 89
M&B FIVE 120
MADDOX Eddie 41
MALTESE JOE 36 37
MANN George 'Duke' 28 40
MANN Johnny 41 127
MARK RAYMOND & THE CROWD 118
MARK TIME & THE COUNTDOWNS 103
MARSH Chalky 118
MARTIN Billy 83
MASON Barry 104 117
MASTERS Greg 61 76 111 119 125 128
MATTHEWS Arthur 23
MAVERICKS 112
MAYFAIR SET 124
McGANN Joe 89
McGINTY Pete 68
McNALLY Bob 116
MEREDITH Alan 106 114
MERRIMEN 101
MICKY HARRIS & THE HAWKS 72 83
MIKE JACKS TRIO 13
MIKE SHERIDAN & THE NIGHTRIDERS 34 56 60 84 115 117 124 127

MILLS Freddie 22
MILLS George 81
MILLS Robert 81
MINNEL Norman 44
MODERNAIRES 27 41 42 53 55 62 64 65 67 74 80 121
MOODY BLUES 30 120 123 126
MOONSHINE 43
MOORE Ralph 68
MORRIS Noel 107
MORTIBOYS Billy 8
MOUNTNEY Dave 68
MOVE 124 127
MUDLARKS 30
MUFF WOODY JAZZ BAND 92
MUNNS Tim 88 96
MURRAY Jimmy 56
MUTCH Ian 'Monk' 110
MYATT Phil 120
MYSTERIES 62 103
NASHVILLES 29
NEAL Johnny 11 12 14 21 23 34 38 85 105 110
NEWMAN Brian 30 42
NEWTON Alan 68
NEWTON Clive 68
NICHOLLS Rob 62 128
NICHOLS Geoff 109
NIGHTHAWKS 15
NIGHTRIDERS 34 56 60 84 92 115 117 119 124 127
NIGNOGS 24 35
NOISY BOYS 15 20 27
OLDACRE Alan 30
OLIVER Pete 61
OLYMPICS 55 110
ONSLOW Jimmy 51 120
OSBORNE John 'Ozzie' 125
OWEN Tommy 15 23 60 75 94
PARAMORE Norrie 95 113 118
PARTRIDGE Mick 43
PAT WAYNE & THE BEACHCOMBERS 118
PAT WAYNE & THE ROCKIN JAYMEN 115
PAT WAYNE'S DELTAS 105
PAWSON Dan 84
PAWSON Maude 84
PEBBLE Graham 'Eddie' 14
PEGG Pat 107
PENNY Pauline 39
PEPLOW Mick 43
PERFECT Christine 44
PETERS Phil 55 79
PHANTOMS 30 36 43 49 59 63 64 95 110
PHILLIPS DANCES 43
PINDER Mick 30 32 50 61 89 109 119 125
POLKA TULK 125
POWELL Jimmy 40 50 52 70 73 77 82 88
POWELL Keith 27 40 51 52 53 57 70 93 104 105 115 116 118
PRESCOTT Johnny 117
PRESS Maurice 81

PRICE Steve 110
PRITCHARD Barry 101
PRITCHARD Dave 34 128
PRYKE Rob 90
PULLEN John 91
PURSUERS 106
QUINTEENOES 21
QUINTON CAPERS 20
QUIRKE Garth 16 60 75
R&B PREACHERS 119
R&B QUARTET 105
RAINBOW BOYS 13 17 29
RAINBOW David 13
RALSTON 90
RAMRODS 40 52
RARE BREED 125
RAVE ONS 35 103
RAY Danny 34 103
RAYMOND Mark 31 103 118
READY STEADY TEDDY 123 124
REBELS 44 45 54 63 76 91 109
REDCAPS 108 114 118
REED Les 98
REGAN Joe 25 26 67 96 108 121
REGAN Mary 'Ma' 26 67 108 114 118
RENEGADES 80
REST 125
RICHARD Cliff 33
RICHES Phil 118
RITTER Mal 105
ROBBY HOOD'S MERRIMEN 101
ROBERTS Dave 27 65
ROBERTS Jeff 105 119
ROBINSON Bunny 118
ROBSON Johnny 22
ROCKIN' BERRIES 45 49 54 63 64 73 77 80 87 96 110 116
121 123
ROCKIN' CHEVROLETS 107 114
ROCKIN' D'FENDERS 93
ROCKIN' JAYMAN 52 105 115
ROCKIN' MODERNAIRES see MODERNAIRES
ROCKIN' SOLITAIRES 81
ROCKING TUXEDOES 30
ROLLER COASTERS 23 30
ROMAD Ray 36
RONNIE & THE SENATORS 80
ROSE Euan 69
ROTUNDAS 103
ROWLANDS John 109
ROY VEARS & THE STRANGERS 103
ROYALS 60 63 75 94 115 117
RUSSELL Tom 28
RYLAND Dennis 31 32 35 43 77 88
SAINT John 110
SAINTS & SINNERS 44
SATELLITES 103
SCHROEDER John 121

SEARCHERS 120
SECUNDA Tony 123
SEELEY Keith 46
SENORITAS 112
SHAKESPEARE John 122
SHANE Johnny 81
SHARPE Brian 10 13 24 27 53 65 105
SHEIL Larry 30
SHERIDAN Mike 34 56 60 84 115 117 124 127
SHEWARD Bob 15 60 61 76 110
SHIP John 79
SHIRLEY Rue 29
SIMPSON Charlie 8 26 78
SINGER John 52 76 110
SMART Keith 40 110 128
SMITH Bob 115 118
SMITH Carl 117
SMITH Colin 40 50 73 117
SMITH Ken 47 85 95
SMITH Roger 55
SMITH Ronnie 80
SMITH Terry 19
SOMBREROS 103
SONNY ROSE ORCHESTRA 8
SOUTHERNERS 122
SPENCER DAVIS GROUP 120 125
SPENCER Roger 34
STAN WHITE BAND The 39
STARKEY Richard 123
STARLINERS 85 110
STEELE Tommy 50
STEVE BRETT & THE MAVERICKS 112
STEVE GIBBONS BAND 127
STEVENS Lee 103
STEVENS Nick 61 101
STIRLING Peter Lee 98 116 124
STOKES Geoff 14
STRANGERS 103
STRAWFORD Mal 31 32 41
STUART Mark 83 85 92 126
SWINGING CHIMES 96
TAYLOR Geoff 11
TAYLOR Maurice 11
TEDDY FOSTER BAND 8
TEMPEST Colin B 102
TERRY & HIS SENORITAS 112
TERRY WALLACE & THE VIKINGS 66
TEX DETHRIDGE & THE GATORS 10 11
THOMAS Ray 44 45 76 91 109 119
THOMPSON Alan 80
THOMPSON Dougie 48 49 54 64 77 81 88 99 110 121
THOMSON Bobby 77 123
THORNTON Walter 31
THUNDERCLAPS 31
TIGER SHARKS 13 29 31
TOM JONES & THE SQUIRES 109
TOMMY BURTON COMBO 95

TOMMY HAWK & THE HATCHETS 22 50
TONY'S SKIFFLE BAND 11
TOOLEY Colin 71
TOVEY Wally 55
TREVOR BORTON & THE EVERGLADES 110 111
TRILLOE Ray 12 17
TUNNICLIFFE Ted 62
TURNER Joe 10
TURTON Geoff 44 96 122
TUXEDOS 61 125
TYLER Mike 33
UGLIES 127
VALENTINE Bobby 40 70 105
VALETS 105 115 116 117
VAUGHAN Ray 19 20 41
VAUGHAN Wally 20
VEARS Roy 103
VIKINGS 19 20 22 28 40 66 70 93 99 104 120 124
VILES Cyril 33 35 36 50 58
VINCE 33 42
VIPERS 22
VIRTUES 47
VIV JONES BAND 39
VYSE Dezi 48 55 68 78 108
WADE Dean 100
WADE Ricky 44
WADEMEN 100
WAKEHAM Billy 39
WALKER Dave 108
WALKER Mick 108
WALLACE Cheryl 70 93
WALLACE Terry 18 22 29 66 70 71 128
WARD Bill 125
WARD Hedley 8

WARWICK Clint 18 40 119 126
WATSON John 47 109
WAYNE Carl 71 93 98 99 120 124 127
WAYNE Pat 20 22 23 25 38 41 46 58 105 115 116 118
WAYNOR Cherry 46
WEBB Pete 109
WEST Mike 101
WHADDLEY Dave 106 107
WHEELAND Dave 'Wongy' 58 87 89
WHEELER Chris 111
WHEELER Ralph 111
WHITE Jimmy 57
WHITE Stan 39
WHITEHOUSE Johnny 41
WILBY Fred 12
WILDCATS 31
WILDE Jimmy 11
WILEMAN Johnny 60
WILLIAMS Tom 30
WILLIAMSON Nicol 27
WINWOOD Mervyn 'Muff' 92 106 125
WINWOOD Steve 92 106 120 125
WITHERS Tony 80
WITHEY Tom 36
WIZARD 127
WOOD Colin 105
WOOD Roy 83 109 124 127
WORRALL Pete 23 30 84
WRIGHT Nigel 69 100
WRIGHT Rodney 69 100
YEATES Brian 72 83 92 126
YEATES John 72 92
YORK Pete 92 106 125
ZENITH Lee 103

LACES

LAS VEGAS COFFEE BAR Summer row 81
LAST CHANCE CAFÉ Aston 38
LESTER'S Wolverhampton 74
LOCARNO BALLROOM Hurst Street 60 102
LONGRIDGE Rubery 55
LUCAS SOCIAL CLUB Hockley 75
LUNCHBOX 43
LYNDON Sheldon 72
MANEY HALL Sutton Coldfield 47 58 87 95
MARLBOROUGH Small Heath 107 108
MARQUEE CLUB Soho London 122
MASQUE BALLROOM Sparkbrook 8
MAYPOLE Warstock 33 56
McKECHNIE'S CANTEEN Aldridge 53
MEM CLUB Tyseley 13 62
MERMAID Sparkhill 11 58
MIDLAND BEAT 108 125
MITCHELLS & BUTLERS 120
MOAT HOUSE Moat Row 85 90 113 115 120
MORRIS CLUB Alum Rock 8
MOTHERS CLUB Erdington 44
MUNTZ PARK 35
NAUTICAL CLUB Dean Street 63
NAVIGATION Bromford 55
NECHELLS BATHS 8
NELSON Spring Hill 20 29
NELSON HOUSE Coventry Road 83
ODEON CINEMA New Street 50
OLDRIDGE RECORD SHOP Selly Oak 59
OPPOSITE LOCK Gas Street 125
ORIOLE STUDIOS 98
PALACE Redditch 54 63 64
PARLOPHONE RECORDS 94 116
PENGUIN CAFÉ 23
PENNS HALL Sutton Coldfield 41
PICCADILLY RECORDS 121
PLAZA BALLROOM Handsworth 25 29 67 69 78 79 80
85 96 108 109
PLAZA Stockland Green 43
PYE RECORDS 114
PYPE HAYES PARK 21
QUEEN MARY BALLROOM Dudley 101
QUEEN'S HEAD Erdington 85
RACKHAMS Department Store 86
RAINBOW SUITE Dale End 117
RAVENSCROFT SOCIAL CLUB Small Heath 82
RCA RECORDS 121
RESERVOIR HOTEL Earlswood 110
RHYTHM UNLIMITED CLUB Hill Street 91
RIDGEWAY DANCE CLUB Hockley Hill 106
RIDOUTS Monument Road 25
RITZ Kings Heath 8 26 64 67 80 96 109 121
ROCK CINEMA Alum Rock 23
ROGER BRUCE RECORD SHOP 27 80
ROOKERY Handsworth 25
RUBERY SOCIAL CLUB 49
SAILORS RETURN Garrison Lane 65
ST IVOR'S CHURCH HALL Sparkhill 30
ST MARGARET'S CHURCH HALL 40
ST STEPHEN'S HALL Pershore Road 24
SALTLEY BATHS 8

SAY MAMA CLUB Sutton Coldfield 47 58 85 87 94
SCALA CINEMA Wolverhampton 42 63 64 74
SELLY PARK LEGION CLUB 35
SHARD END BRITISH LEGION 55 68
SHAREHOLADERS Aston 114
SHELDON MUSIC Coventry Road 23
SHERWOOD ROOMS Nottingham 101
SHIP Highley 18
SHIRLEY ANNEXE 56 81
SHIRLEY CARNIVAL 30
SHUSTOKE VILLAGE HALL 15
SICILIO COFFEE BAR Five Ways 74 84
SMOKEY JOE'S TRANSPORT CAFÉ Northfield 73
SNACKERIE Hill Street 57
SOLIHULL CARNIVAL 21
SOLIHULL CIVIC HALL 90
SPRING HILL ICE RINK 68
SPRINGFIELD Sparkhill 8 90 114
STAFFORDSHIRE VOLUNTEER Wolverhampton 39
STAN THE VAN Sparkbrook 87
STAR BALLROOM Burton 85
STAR BALLROOM Sparkhill 90
STAR CLUB Hamburg 85
STATION Brownhills 75
STATION Selly Oak 31
STATUS RECORDS Tyseley 64
STELLA'S BAR Aston 14
STONEHOUSE GANG YOUTH CLUB 51
STREETLEY YOUTH CLUB 62
SWAN Washwood Heath 29 60
SWAN Yarley 8 42 65 67 80
SYDENHAM Small Heath 43 63
TABOO CLUB Stirchley 36 99
TAMWORTH ASSEMBLY ROOMS 85
THIMBLEMILL BATHS 8
TILE CROSS YOUTH CLUB 76
TONY'S BALLROOM Hurst Street 8 27
TOP TEN CLUB Hamburg 75 94
TOP TWENTY CLUB Peckham 94
TOWN HALL Birmingham 13 20 21 22 25 52 76
TOWN HALL Brierley Hill 39
TOWN HALL Ludlow 68
TOWN HALL Pembridge 68
TYBURN HOUSE Erdington 90
UNITY CLUB Summer Lane 18
VICTORIA Small Heath 26
VINCENT HALL Ladywood 74
WEST END BALLROOM Suffolk Street 28 59 85 109 118
WHEATLEY'S SHOP Golden Hillock Road 30
WHEATSHEAF Sheldon 85
WHISKY A GO-GO CLUB Navigation Street 120
WHITE SWAN Washwood Heath 60
WOLSELEY Drews Lane 8 28 29
WOODROFFE'S John Bright Street 34 103
WYCHBOLD HOTEL Sutton Coldfield 43
YARDLEY'S Snow Hill 103
YMCA Bordesley 40
YMCA Erdington 31
ZAMBEZIE COFFEE BAR Broad Street 46
ZISSMANS Bull Street 43
ZISSMANS Dale End 89